Sunset
Chinese
Cook Book

By the Editors of Sunset Books and Sunset Magazine

Lane Publishing Co. • Menlo Park, California

Good Chinese cooking begins in the market. Adjust your menu or recipe to take advantage of the freshest vegetables available to you.

Sunset went to Hong Kong & China...

... where professional chefs and home cooks underscored what we had learned from Chinese-American food experts here: The success of Chinese cooking comes from the use of basic techniques rather than exotic ingredients. For centuries Chinese cooks have delighted in preparing good food. With this cook book you can easily prepare the best of Chinese food—from Peking, Shanghai, Szechwan, Hunan, and Canton—and enjoy yourself immensely in the process.

We wish to extend a special thank you to those who helped with the research for this book: Loretta Cheung, Alice Li, Lucy Lo, Willie Mark, Marjorie Tsin Wai Ming, Suzanna Pang, all of Hong Kong; Clement Kwong, China Grove Restaurant; Chef Show Kang Wang, Yu Shan Restaurant; Hong Kong Tourist Association; and Food Street of Hong Kong.

Edited by Janeth Johnson Nix

Special Consultant:
Linda Anusasananan
Assistant Editor, Sunset Magazine

Design:
Cynthia Hanson

Photography:
Tom Wyatt
with Lynne B. Morrall

Illustrations:
Alan May

Editor, Sunset Books: David E. Clark

Third Printing October 1981

Covers: Kung Pao Shrimp (page 46), stir-fried broccoli and mushrooms (page 72), and fresh mandarin oranges is our front cover subject; back cover shows Caramel Fried Apples (page 90). Photographs by Tom Wyatt

Contents

Special Features

Getting Started

You don't easily forget good Chinese food. You may not be able to recall it by name or identify the ingredients, but the delight lingers and you know you've eaten something delicious and wonderful.

This book is for those who want to enjoy the best of Chinese food at home. If you're new to Chinese cooking, you'll find all the help and encouragement you need to make your first try a smashing success. If you're an old hand at cooking Chinese food, you'll recognize some old favorites and discover many new regional treasures from Peking, Shanghai, Szechwan, Hunan, and Canton.

The dishes are not difficult to make and many can be prepared in easy cook-ahead stages. Few exotic ingredients are called for. Happily, our increased interest in things Chinese has brought canned sauces and seasonings—once found only in Oriental food stores—to the shelves of well-stocked supermarkets.

Whenever possible we give easy-to-find substitutes. If you read over a recipe and find that you lack a small quantity of a special seasoning, don't hesitate to cook without it. The flavor may not be quite the same, but you'll still capture the essence of the dish. Chinese cooking is more a matter of techniques than ingredients anyway, and you can apply techniques wherever good vegetables and meat are available.

But why go to the trouble of cooking your own Chinese food? Different cooks will give different reasons. One may say it adds variety to everyday meals; another may claim it lends verve and drama to entertaining. It also provides a relief for the budget. With Chinese food you can eat less and still eat well. But most important of all, it is such a pleasure to relax and thoroughly enjoy good Chinese food. The Chinese sum it up well: "Shut out your worries and open your chopsticks."

The Beginnings

When you cook Chinese food you can feel a sense of continuity. Each step you take and each sequence you follow has been repeated thousands of times before by thousands of cooks—and for very logical reasons.

Over the centuries, many a famine has swept China. At the same time, the Chinese have been faced with a large population, a relatively small portion of land suitable for cultivation, and a limited supply of fuel. As a result, they have been continually forced to look for new ways to sustain life.

They developed methods of cooking that required little fuel, and they explored everything edible or that could be made edible. When near starvation they'd try anything, but it had to be good. A family might have only a dish of fried grasshoppers, yet a simple but tasty sauce—maybe even two or three—would go with it. And it is this reverence for food, even a preoccupation with it, which was, and still is, the strong force shaping Chinese cooking.

In addition, the chefs of the great dynasties were constantly challenged to new and exotic heights by the demands of the royal kitchens and leisure class. And this tradition of innovation is instilled in today's chefs as well. The result is a blending of savoriness, economy, and style in a cuisine that tantalizes even the most discriminating tastes.

Regional Influences

Since China is a vast country with a great range of climate and terrain, it is only natural that its cuisine evolved from regional styles. From the earliest times, each region developed its own traditions based on locally available ingredients and flavor preferences. As means of transportation and communication developed and food ideas moved beyond their native areas, many recipes retained their regional character, but the characteristics of others were lost or diffused. That is why we have identified some recipes in this book as regional specialties but not others—they are the ones that have been woven into the total cuisine.

Not all food historians would agree, but most categorize Chinese cooking by four major styles: northern, which revolves around the cuisine of the capital city of Peking and the Shantung province; eastern or coastal, influenced by the cosmopolitan character of the cities of Shanghai and Hangchow; southeastern or Cantonese, the type of Chinese food first introduced into the United States; and southwestern, home of food from Szechwan and Hunan.

Some Chinese restaurants specialize in what is termed "mandarin cooking." A mandarin was a senior official of the Chinese Empire ruled from Peking. Consequently, "mandarin cooking" connotes northern Chinese dishes for the palates of the select.

Peking Style in the North

Being the center of government and trade during so much of

China's history, the northern city of Peking naturally became a focus of culinary, artistic, and intellectual activity as well. Highly imaginative culinary art was developed to honor official Chinese visitors to the Court, and when China opened its doors to foreigners in 1844, this sophistication in Peking was further developed.

Today, as in the past, the Peking cuisine is characterized by sweet and sour sauces, wine-based cooking stocks, hoisin sauce, garlic, sesame oil, green onions, yeasty doughs, and the generous use of soy sauce. Depending on the dish, the seasonings can be mild or strong.

Wheat is the staple grain of the north and it appears in noodles, dumplings, and marvelous breads. Peking duck is probably the most famous northern dish, but there are other well-known specialties. One favorite is Mongolian hot pot, a type of fondue in which slices of lamb and vegetables are cooked in a rich stock at the table. Also popular are artistically arranged appetizer cold plates that contain tidbits of meat, poultry, and seafood.

Shanghai-style Cooking

The Yangtse River, rising in the Tibetan Highlands and emptying into the East China Sea, flows through the heartland of China. Near the mouth of the Yangtse is Shanghai, a major industrial and trading center and the largest city of China. The cuisine of this fertile river valley takes its name from this city.

The cosmopolitan Shanghai style is both subtle and complex. Soups, vegetables, and seafood dishes are often light and delicate, meat and poultry dishes rich and savory. Wheat noodles and rice are important staples, while a liberal use of sugar, soy, and wine are the trademarks of Shanghai-style cooking.

Though many Shanghai-style dishes served in restaurants call for highly complex cooking techniques, the recipes in this book reflect the simpler red-cooked or braised dishes that are famous throughout the area. It is the dark brown soy sauce used in the broth that turns the food a brownish red. And because each cook has an individualized master recipe, there are dozens of subtle variations of this technique which adapts so well to meat, poultry, and seafood.

The Cooking of Canton

Of all the styles of Chinese cooking, Cantonese food is probably the most familiar to Americans. The cuisine takes its name from the port city of Canton, capital of Kwangtung province in southeastern China.

From this area came the 19th century waves of immigrants who introduced Chinese cooking to the United States. Many of the Chinese restaurants that first opened in America served not what they thought was best, but what they thought would appeal most to the local clientele. Usually this was simple, basic Cantonese food, often enjoyed as much for its low price as its taste appeal.

In recent years, with the opening of more regional Chinese restaurants in this country, Cantonese food has lost some of its attraction. If you have not ventured far beyond chop suey or chow mein, you may even think the food is unexciting and dull. But when you take time to explore the many delicious Cantonese dishes, you realize that this cooking perhaps shows the greatest variety and depth of any of the regional Chinese cuisines.

This may be due in part to the fact that southeastern China has an unusual abundance of good food to cook. Its moist, tropical climate provides a long growing season for rice, vegetables, and fruits, and the 1000-mile coastline is rich with fish and shellfish. So Cantonese cooks know that fresh ingredients need few frills: their food is light and generally mild, with an emphasis on pure natural flavors.

Through the centuries, the cooking of Canton has been influenced by migrations from northern China during times of political turmoil. It was also influenced by commerce with the Portuguese, Dutch, and other Western traders who first established contact with the Chinese. They introduced

Map of China

such foods as peanuts, corn, tomatoes, and white potatoes.

Though Cantonese cooks use a full range of cooking techniques, over the years they have become world famous for their wide variety of stir-fried dishes. They are also experts at preparing a multitude of snack foods, from fried noodles to steamed dim sum. Their favorite seasonings include black bean sauce, oyster sauce, and lobster sauce.

Szechwan & Hunan

Completely opposite to the delicate flavors of Cantonese cooking are the robust, spicy hot dishes of Szechwan and Hunan.

This food from southwestern China is hot for several reasons—the semitropical climate is favorable for growing chiles and other spices, and the proximity to Burma, Pakistan, and India has influenced the use of curry, chiles, and highly seasoned condiments.

Classic southwest dishes usually have two tastes—the initial sting of hot peppers and the more mellow aftertaste of sweet, sour, and salty flavors. The hot peppers are used in many forms—whole, crushed, powdered, and in oil. Despite their heat, they give zest to a dish without overpowering it.

Of the two styles—Hunan and Szechwan—Hunan is considered hotter. But both of these cuisines have their exceptions, too. Many banquet-style dishes are often bland and somewhat light.

Basic Equipment

The surprising things about the kitchen in an average Chinese home are its simplicity and small size—one or two burners for cooking, a short counter and sink, and a small cupboard for condiments. One wonders how such a variety of food can come from such a small space. Many Chinese restaurants, too, are able to turn out dozens of orders continuously with what appears to be minimal equipment. The secret lies in the versatility of the equipment.

The Wok

For the Chinese, the bowl-shaped wok is basic. With it they can use almost any cooking method and cook almost any ingredient. While it is possible for you to prepare any recipe in this book with your regular kitchen equipment, a wok will make the job easier and more fun.

For stir-frying and deep-frying, a wok uses less oil than a frying pan because there is less area to be covered. As a bonus, the high sloping sides of a wok confine any splatters to the pan. With the addition of a lid and a rack or bamboo steaming trays, the wok can double as a steamer.

For stir-frying, a heavy-gauge carbon steel wok is best because it conducts heat better than one made of aluminum, stainless steel, or copper. With an electric wok, the temperature drops when you add food and it takes a few seconds to reheat the wok. Because of this you need to cook food in somewhat smaller batches to maintain a constant high heat.

Woks come in a variety of sizes, but for most home cooking the 14-inch-diameter wok is the most practical. You can always stir-fry a small amount of food in a large wok, but you can't stir-fry a large amount in a small one. The style of handle—two metal ones or a long wooden one—is simply a matter of choice.

Traditional Chinese woks have round bottoms and they sit in a ring for stability. This works well on a gas range. If you cook on an electric range, you'll have better results if you use one of the modern, flat-bottomed woks and place it directly on the burner. On a gas range you can change the temperature of your wok instantly by turning the flame up or down. It takes longer to heat or cool a pan on an electric range, but you can still cool your wok instantly by simply removing it from the heating element for a moment if it is getting too hot.

Before you use a carbon steel wok it should be seasoned. Wash it with sudsy water, then dry it by placing it directly over high heat on your range for a minute or two. Next, rub the inside with a paper towel dipped in salad oil, then remove the excess oil with a clean towel. After each use, wash the wok and dry it on the range element. If the wok is not completely dry it will rust.

A dome-shaped lid may come with a wok, or you can buy one separately. It is helpful in stir-frying and necessary when you use your wok as a steamer. Three other accessories you might consider are a ladle, a long-handled spatula designed to fit the curve of the wok, and a brass wire skimmer—good for removing food from hot oil. You may find alternatives to any or all of these in your own kitchen that will work just as well.

Slicing & Dicing

The second basic piece of equipment in a Chinese kitchen is a cleaver, and with it, of course, a surface for cutting. The cleaver is used for slicing and mincing, hacking and chopping; it also serves as a scoop to lift pieces from the cutting board to the pan.

Cleavers come in three weights. The medium weight is best for all-purpose use, but it's a good idea to hold one in your hand to get the feel of it before you buy one. They are made of stainless steel and carbon steel. The latter holds its edge best. Like a carbon steel wok, it should be thoroughly dried after each use to prevent rusting. If you choose not to use a cleaver, you can use a good knife with a wedge-shaped blade.

To use with the cleaver, some cooks like a thick, round, wooden chopping block. A wooden cutting board about 1 inch thick may be easier to handle since it is light enough to pick up and wash after use.

For very sound reasons, the

Cook Shanghai Duck (page 53) ahead for a festive party entrée. To eat, tuck pieces of succulent meat inside of Steamed Buns (page 87).

Chinese are particular about cutting. They feel that a dish is more pleasing when the shapes are evenly matched. Even more important, ingredients cut the same size will cook in the same length of time.

Throughout this book, we give cutting directions for the traditional presentation, but if you're in a hurry, there's no harm in changing the rules. If a recipe calls for matchstick pieces of vegetables, you can cut them in slices instead, provided all pieces are thinly sliced for even cooking.

Many firm vegetables can be neatly sliced with a food processor. You lose some of the beauty of the traditionally cut shapes, but there may be times when you are willing to trade beauty for speed. For many of the mincing and fine chopping tasks, a processor works well.

Steaming Equipment

If you have a wok, you can convert it to a steamer by using a metal or wooden rack made especially for the wok (or just a round cake rack) along with the wok lid. Or you can use stacked bamboo baskets that you set inside the wok, allowing several dishes to steam on different layers at once. The wok lid won't fit with steamer baskets; you must purchase a special lid to use with them.

There are also several types of steamers you can buy; or you can improvise one with a large pan, a lid, and a support to hold a dish or rack off the bottom of the pan. For the large pan you can use an electric or regular wide frying pan with a domed lid, or any large deep kettle with a lid. The lid should be 1 to 2 inches above the cooking food so steam can circulate.

The supports to hold food above the water vary, depending on whether you steam the food in a dish or just on a perforated tray or on a cake rack. Acting as a shield between the food and the water, a dish does not have to be much above the water—it can be supported with canning jar rings or

7-ounce tuna cans with both ends removed. A perforated rack or tray must be supported at least 2 inches above the simmering water so that the water does not bubble up onto the food (see illustration below). Taller cans, such as several 1-pound cans with both ends removed, make good supports.

Cooking Techniques

The Chinese use many cooking techniques and most are familiar —braising, steaming, roasting, deep-frying. The one that stands apart and is uniquely Chinese is stir-frying, a method that seldom takes more than a few minutes to complete.

Our photographs on page 10 illustrate this technique step by step. On page 71 we discuss stir-frying in greater detail. We urge you to read these directions several times before beginning to cook. Our recipes give cooking times to serve as a guide, but you may find that your times vary slightly because of the intensity of your heat source, the size of your pan, and the thinness of your slices. You'll feel more comfortable if you can visualize the sequence of steps rather than be concerned with exact minutes and seconds.

Stir-frying has only one prerequisite for success: you must have everything ready before you start to cook. Once you begin to stir-fry a dish, you won't have time to stop and look for a missing ingredient or to mix a sauce.

The technique is easy to master and, like all Chinese cooking techniques, open to improvisation. In many recipes in this book you will see the Chinese character 注意 which means "note this." We have used the character to indicate recipes in which one or two ingredients have been changed to create a new dish.

Seasonings & Ingredients

You don't need to shop far from home to begin Chinese cooking. Many recipes in this book can be made with a few basic sauces and seasonings available in markets everywhere. Ginger, green onion, soy sauce, and sherry are the most essential. Then, as you try a wider range of dishes, you may wish to visit a Chinese market for the more special items.

The photograph on page 15 and the list that follows will help you identify the familiar and not-so-familiar ingredients.

Abalone is a distinctively flavored mollusk sold fresh, dried, and canned. Our recipes use only canned abalone. In this form it is ready to slice thin for appetizers, add to soup, or stir-fry. You cook it only long enough to heat through; overcooking makes it tough and rubbery. If you do not use the whole can at one time, drain and save the liquid for soup, place the abalone in a jar, and cover with cold water; then cover the jar and refrigerate for as long as 1 week, changing water daily.

Bamboo shoots are available canned. Look for sliced bamboo shoots when a recipe calls for slices or matchstick pieces; look for whole bamboo shoots when a recipe calls for diced pieces. Light yellow in color, they are tender and fibrous with a little sweetness that comes alive when cooked. Place extra bamboo shoots in a glass jar, cover with water, add lid, and refrigerate for as long as 10 days, changing water daily.

Bean curd (tofu). For a complete description, see page 69.

Fermented black beans are small fermented black beans preserved in salt. They are sold in small plastic bags in three styles: plain, flavored with garlic, or flavored with ginger. Used for sauces in combination with fresh garlic and ginger, they have a very pungent flavor for their size. Place in a sieve and rinse with water before using. Store beans in a tightly covered jar in a cool, dry place.

Bean sauce (brown bean sauce, Chinese bean sauce, yellow bean sauce) is a thick brown sauce made from fermented soybeans, salt, flour, and sugar. It is sold in two forms—regular bean sauce, which contains whole beans, and ground bean sauce, which has a smoother texture. It is available in cans or jars. After opening, transfer to a covered jar and refrigerate.

A variation of this is the *sweet* bean sauce used in Szechwan-style cooking. If you can't find it, substitute hoisin sauce.

Hot bean sauce (Szechwan hot bean sauce) is a spicy, hot sauce made from soybeans, kidney beans, flour, chiles, salt, sesame oil, sugar, and pepper. Use sparingly in cooking or as a dipping sauce for crisp food. Sold in cans, it should be transferred after opening to a covered jar and may be refrigerated for up to 3 months. If unavailable, substitute a crumbled, small, dry, hot chile pepper, for each 1 teaspoon of bean sauce.

Bean sprouts are 2 to 3-inch-long sprouted mung beans. They are sold fresh, either packaged or loose. Purchased in top condition, they will keep in a perforated plastic bag in the refrigerator for as long as 4 days. Translucent and crisp, they add crunch to any dish. Bean sprouts are also available in cans, but they lack the crisp texture.

Bean threads (translucent, cellophane, or shining noodles) are made from ground mung beans and are sold dried in packages weighing 2 ounces to 1 pound.

Though they are called noodles, they are considered a vegetable product. Before they are cooked, they look like stiff nylon fishing line, but they puff up crisp when dropped into hot oil (see page 82). Or you can cover them with warm water for 30 minutes to soften, then simmer in soups or stir-fry with meat or vegetables.

Bok choy (Chinese white cabbage) is a tender-crisp, sweet, very mild vegetable consisting of a clump of snow-white stalks ending in wide, dark green leaves.

Dried chestnuts are shelled, blanched, and dried; they are sold by weight in Oriental markets. Before simmering with meat or poultry, cover with hot water, let stand for 1 hour, then drain. Simmer in water to cover for 1 hour.

Chile peppers—the kind used in the recipes in this book—are dried and packaged by American spice companies, so they are readily available. Use them whole or break them in half and shake out the

Thirst quenchers

When you take time to serve good food, it's worth taking time to match the food with just the right beverage. Tea, of course, is traditional with Chinese food, and the Chinese enjoy every kind of tea imaginable.

No matter what kind of tea is used, though, most Chinese tea experts agree that Americans and other English-speaking people brew their tea too strong. Any tea, no matter how fine, will taste harsh and bitter if it is too strong.

Test a tea that is new to you. Decide what proportion of leaves to water tastes best. The proportion varies with the type of tea and may range from a heaping spoonful of tea leaves for each cup of water to only 1 teaspoon for 6 cups of water.

To brew tea properly, bring water just to a brisk boil. Pour some of the boiling water into the teapot; when the pot is warm, pour the water out. Then add tea to the pot and pour in the appropriate amount of boiling water. Cover and steep for at least 3 minutes before serving. You can brew more than one pot of tea from the same leaves; in fact, some people believe the second or third brewing is better than the first.

You may prefer to serve another beverage with the meal, though, and end with tea. If your choice is wine, you can overlook the formalized rules frequently followed with wines. Chinese food, with its contrasts of hot, spicy, sweet, and sour flavors all served in one meal, tends to dominate the complexity of many varietal wines.

A slightly sweet, fruity white wine—such as a Riesling, French Colombard, Gewürztraminer, Chenin Blanc, Green Hungarian, or Sylvaner — or a Rosé seems to provide the perfect complement for Chinese food.

Sparkling cider and sweetened clear sparkling soda are other good choices, as are ginger ale and lemon or orange soda. If your menu features spicy hot food, you may even prefer to serve beer or lemonade to quench the fire.

The Stir-fry Technique

1. *Have everything ready before you start to cook asparagus chicken. Heat wok; add oil. When oil is hot but not smoking, swirl around pan. Cook seasonings quickly until fragrant.*

2. *Add chicken to pan and spread out in an even layer. After 30 seconds, stir and tumble to cook evenly. If chicken sticks, scrape pan with spatula. Remove chicken when opaque.*

3. *Heat more oil. Add vegetables and stir at once to coat. Add a spoonful of water; cover pan and steam vegetables briefly. Add a few more drops water if pan appears dry.*

4. *Return chicken to pan. Stir cooking sauce to reblend cornstarch. Pour sauce into pan around edges so sauce heats and cooks quickly. Stir as sauce thickens.*

seeds. They are also sold as crushed red pepper; one teaspoon is equivalent to roughly 1 small, dry, hot chile pepper.

Chili oil is sold in both Chinese and Japanese markets, or you can make your own (see page 37).

Chinese cabbage (napa cabbage) is a solid, oblong head of white celerylike stalks ending in frilly, pale green leaves. It is mild, delicate, and crisp-textured.

Chinese five-spice is a blend of ground cloves, fennel, licorice root, cinnamon, and star anise. It is bottled by American spice companies and readily available.

Chinese mustard is premixed and sold in a jar for use as a dip for shrimp, roast pork, spareribs, or any time you want a hot, spicy flavor. You can also make your own (see page 37).

Chinese noodles (mein) are made of wheat flour, with or without egg. They may simply be labeled "mein," or the word may not be on the package at all. They come dried, or fresh in packages of looped or curly bundles. As a substitute, use any fresh or dried thin noodle or thin spaghetti.

Chinese sausages (lop cheong) are compact links about 6 inches long, with a slightly sweet and spicy flavor. They are a pork sausage and must be cooked before eating. Steam for 15 minutes, then serve with rice and a dipping sauce of mustard, or slice and stir-fry with other ingredients. Refrigerate for as long as 1 month, or freeze for longer storage.

Fresh coriander (Chinese parsley or cilantro) is a green broadleaf parsley, but it doesn't taste a thing like regular parsley. Powerful and pungent, it is used in small quantities to garnish many dishes.

Dried black fungus (wood ear or cloud ear) is a small, crinkly dried fungus, about 1 inch long, that is sold by weight in Oriental markets. It expands dramatically when soaked. Before cooking, cover with warm water and soak for 30 minutes, then cut off the hard

knobby part. Slice or chop to add a light, crisp texture. Store unused dried fungus in a cool dry place.

Garlic is an integral part of Chinese cooking. A whole head can be minced with a food processor to keep on hand for instant use: Separate into cloves and cut off each end. Using the metal blade, process one head at a time, unpeeled; then refrigerate in a covered jar for as long as 1 week. One teaspoon minced garlic equals 1 large clove.

To chop and peel a single clove, cut off each end, then crush clove with the side of a cleaver or heavy knife blade. Discard the paperlike peel and continue chopping until minced.

Fresh ginger, indispensable to Chinese cooking, is a gnarled-looking light brown root that is hot and nippy. Buy it in small quantities, as a little goes a long way. When a recipe calls for minced or grated ginger, you needn't peel it.

Store ginger in a cool, dry place. For longer storage, you can use one of several methods: Freeze the ginger; then, without thawing, cut off as much as you need, and grate, slice, or chop it. Or peel a large piece, place it in a jar, and cover with dry sherry; cover and refrigerate for as long as 3 months, using it as needed. (You can recycle the sherry by using it in recipes when a light ginger flavor is desired.) Like garlic, ginger can also be minced in the food processor, a large portion at a time, then covered and refrigerated for as long as 1 week. If fresh ginger is unavailable, leave it out of the recipe—ground or candied ginger make poor substitutes.

Pickled ginger comes in jars. The long shreds of ginger, dyed red, are eaten as a garnish or used in sweet-sour sauce.

Ginkgo nuts are the small beige fruit of the ginkgo tree. Most easily found canned, they are served as appetizers and used in soups, braised dishes, and vegetarian dishes. After opening, place unused nuts in a jar with water, then

cover and refrigerate for as long as 2 weeks, changing water daily.

Hoisin sauce is a thick, smooth, brownish red sauce made from soybeans, flour, sugar, vinegar, and spices. Mildly sweet, it is used in cooking or as a table condiment. Available in cans or jars, it should be refrigerated after opening. It will keep for months under refrigeration in a covered glass jar.

Kumquats are small, oval, orange-colored citrus fruit with a sweet-tart flavor. Sometimes available fresh, they are usually packed in syrup in jars or cans. They should be refrigerated after opening.

Dried lily buds (golden needles or tiger lily buds) are pale gold lily buds about 2 to 3 inches long. Before using, soak them in warm water for 30 minutes; pick off the hard tips before stir-frying.

Lotus seeds are hard, tan seeds of the lotus root, available dried or canned. Cover dried seeds with warm water and let stand for 30 minutes; drain, then simmer in water for 30 minutes before adding to soup for the final 30 minutes of cooking.

Lychees are a sweet, fragrant fruit sold fresh, dried, or canned. You can peel dried lychees and eat them like raisins or prunes. After opening canned lychees, refrigerate them in their own syrup in a covered container.

Dried mushrooms have a firm texture and woodsy perfume when they are cooked. They come in several sizes in packages weighing up to 4 ounces. Before cooking, soak them in warm water for at least 30 minutes. Always cut away the stems after soaking and squeeze the mushrooms dry before slicing.

Oyster sauce is a thick, brown, bottled sauce with a rich, subtle oyster flavor. It is used in stir-fried dishes in place of soy sauce or along with it; it is also used as a table condiment. Refrigerate for as long as 3 months after opening.

Pickled mixed vegetables (sweet mixed ginger or sub gum) are a

Entertaining Chinese-style at home

With their passion for variety, the Chinese don't limit a meal to one regional style of cooking. A meal that starts with a cold plate prepared in the style of Peking might easily end with Cantonese-style noodles.

To get you started, here are six menus that don't follow strict tradition but do make memorable Chinese meals for Western-style entertaining. As you build your repertory and sharpen your skills, you'll find that the best menu for you is a blend of what excites you most, what looks fresh in the market that day, and what you can improvise with the leftovers you have on hand.

Appetizer Party

The length of this menu may look a bit ambitious, yet everything but the shrimp toast can be prepared several days in advance. You can assemble the shrimp toast up to 8 hours ahead, then deep-fry it quickly at the last minute in an electric frying pan. Serve the food Chinese-style on platters in the center of the table. Provide your guests with small plates and chopsticks or forks so they can sample each dish, one by one. All together it is filling enough to make a meal for eight to ten people.

Star Anise Tongue (page 17)
Marinated Abalone (page 17)
White Cut Chicken with Spicy Peanut Sauce (page 48)
Shrimp Toast or Crab Pillows (page 22)
Cold-stirred Lima Beans (page 74)
Sesame Eggplant Salad (page 77)
Marinated Carrots & Snow Peas (page 77)
Cold Spiced Cabbage (page 79)
White Wine (page 9)

A Savory Supper

Everything in this lighthearted menu for four people can be prepared ahead. To serve, all you need to do is boil the won ton for 5 minutes and pour dressing on the salad.

Cold Spiced Shrimp (page 60)
Won Ton Dumplings with Spicy Peanut Sauce (page 88)
Sprout & Cress Salad (page 77)
Anise Pear Compote (page 93)

Szechwan-style Dinner

This menu for four people calls for two stir-fried dishes. But you can cook the bean threads first in a frying pan, then cover and keep them warm while you stir-fry the chicken.

Pork & Preserved Turnip Soup (page 27)
Bean Threads with Hot Bean Sauce (page 82)
Kung Pao Chicken (page 45)   Steamed Rice (page 80)
Sprout & Cucumber Salad (page 79)
Beer or Sparkling Cider
Fresh Fruit

Cantonese Company Meal

The chicken in this menu for six people can be cooked a day ahead. The day of the party, start the rice and soup first. Cook the bean curd in a frying pan, then let the accompanying vegetables simmer in the seasoned stock while you stir-fry the pork.

Abalone & Mustard Green Soup (page 28)
White Cut Chicken with Sweet Sesame Sauce (page 48)
Bean Curd with Vegetables (page 65)
Cashew Pork (page 36)   Steamed Rice (page 80)
Almond Cream (page 92)

Shanghai Duck Dinner

Two dishes in this menu for four people require steaming, but you steam the clams first to serve as an appetizer before you resteam the buns. The buns, duck, and soup can be prepared ahead and reheated while you stir-fry the vegetable.

Pork-stuffed Clams (page 19)
Shrimp with Tomato Soup (page 25)
Shanghai Duck (page 53)   Steamed Buns (page 87)
Stir-fried Broccoli or Cabbage (page 72)
Fresh Fruit   Sesame Cookies (page 93)

A Company Meal

A whole steamed fish, or fillets, is the highlight of this delicious dinner for six people. Start the rice first, then prepare the soup and keep it on low heat after adding the egg whites. Stir-fry the beef 5 minutes before the fish finishes steaming.

Chicken & Corn Soup (page 28)
Steamed Fish (page 56)   Steamed Rice (page 80)
Asparagus Beef with Black Bean Sauce (page 45)
Ice Cream with Lychee Sauce (page 93)

combination of ginger and vegetables preserved with a sugar and vinegar syrup. Sold in jars, they can be eaten cold as a relish or used to make a sweet-sour sauce. Refrigerate for as long as 3 months after opening.

Plum sauce (duck sauce) is a thick, sweet, pungent condiment made from plums, chiles, sugar, vinegar, and spices. It is most frequently used as a dipping sauce. Available in cans or jars, it can be refrigerated in a covered jar for as long as three months after opening. You can also make your own (see page 53).

Quail eggs are sold hard-cooked and shelled, in cans of various sizes. The small can contains about 6 eggs, the large can about 30. Drain and serve as an appetizer, or use as a garnish for soups.

Rice sticks (rice noodles or mai fun) are dried, opaque, white, thin noodles made of ground rice and sold in packages of various weights. Deep-fry them for a garnish (see page 82) or soak them briefly in water, then use in soup or noodle dishes.

Sesame oil is a golden brown, aromatic oil made from toasted sesame seeds. It is used in small quantities, more as a seasoning than for cooking. Many Chinese chefs keep it in a plastic dispenser —or spouted oil can—so they can squirt a few drops into a dish just before serving. It can be refrigerated indefinitely after opening.

Sesame seeds need to be toasted to bring out their sweet nutlike flavor: place them in an ungreased frying pan and cook over low heat, shaking pan frequently, until seeds turn golden and begin to pop (about 2 minutes).

Dried shrimp are tiny, shelled and salted, dried shrimp used in small quantities to flavor soups, vegetables, bean curd, and meat dishes. Soak them in warm water for 30 minutes before using them in cooking. Sold in small plastic bags, they should be repacked in a tightly covered jar; stored in

a cool, dry place they will keep indefinitely.

Snow peas (edible-pod peas, sugar peas, or Chinese pea pods) are available fresh or frozen. They are crisp, flat, bright green, tender pods with tiny, underdeveloped peas inside. Before cooking fresh snow peas, snap off each end and pull the strings straight down the pod sides. Our recipes call for fresh snow peas. If you buy them frozen, cook them just long enough to heat through. If you enjoy gardening, look for the seeds in Oriental markets or nurseries and plant in late fall for a spring harvest.

Soy sauce is a dark, savory, salty sauce made from soybeans, wheat flour, yeast, salt, and sugar. It is one of the most versatile and frequently used sauces in Chinese cooking. The saltiness varies from brand to brand; imported soy sauce is definitely best. Chinese cooks use three kinds—light, dark, and black—singly or combined to achieve different results. Japanese soy, a slightly sweeter cross between the light and dark, may be used with good results. Because of its wide availability, we have used Japanese soy sauce to prepare the recipes in this book. Contrary to popular belief, good Chinese food is not swimming in soy sauce. Use it with restraint to provide the right saltiness and depth of flavor.

Star anise is a dry, brown, licorice-flavored, star-shaped seed sold by weight. It is used in soups, braised meats, and poultry.

Szechwan peppercorns (fagara), sold by weight, are tiny, reddish brown peppercorns sheathed in a flowerlike husk. They have a mildly hot taste and pleasing pungent aroma. They are often dry-roasted before using: place peppercorns in an ungreased frying pan and cook, shaking pan frequently, over medium heat until aromatic; cool, then crush with a mortar and pestle or rolling pin, or leave whole. To make a salt-pepper mix, see page 37.

Szechwan preserved turnip (Szechwan preserved vegetables or Szechwan preserved mustard) consists of gnarled chunks of turnip preserved with salt, chiles, and spices, and sold in cans, jars, and plastic bags. Rinse off the red pickling spice before using, then slice thin and serve as part of a cold plate, or cut in shreds or mince to add flavor to soups and meat and vegetable dishes. After using, refrigerate in a covered jar—it will keep for as long as 3 months.

Vinegar is used for cooking and as a table condiment. The Chinese use four main types—white, sweet, red, and black. All are made from fermented rice and are milder than most American vinegars. If unavailable, substitute any good red or white wine vinegar.

Water chestnuts are crisp and crunchy with sweet flavor. They are peeled, packed in water, and canned. After opening, cover with water and refrigerate. They will keep for as long as 2 weeks if you change the water daily. Fresh water chestnuts are available at certain times of the year in Chinese markets. To prepare them, peel off the brown skin, then use in cooking.

Winter melon is sold whole or in pieces by the pound. It is a large, melon-shaped green squash of varying sizes with a powdery white wax on the skin. The pulp is translucent and white when cooked.

Putting It Together

Few of us would care to undertake a multicourse Chinese meal for a crowd—even the Chinese order their lavish banquets in restaurants. You'll enjoy yourself more, and not become worn out in the process, if you make yourself acquainted with individual recipes in this book first. Serve a single glittering main dish or just an unusual appetizer or a crisp-tender vegetable or a light soup as part of your regular meal. Then, as you cook and become familiar with the techniques, you'll surely want to stage a complete Chinese meal for guests. The results are too good not to share.

Much has been written about how to compose a Chinese meal. Some guides say you should include a soup, a meat, a poultry, a fish, a vegetable, rice, and so on. Others plan a menu around cooking techniques—one dish steamed, one stir-fried, one deep-fried, one roasted, one braised.

Ideally, variety is what you strive for—the contrast of sweet and sour, spicy and cool, subtle and strong, silky and chewy, soft and crisp, pale and richly colored—and the only way to achieve it is to serve a number of separate dishes.

Restaurants use this rule of thumb: One dish for each person, plus rice and tea. For two or three this is easily achieved; but if your guest list expands to eight, it could be overwhelming. You don't have to follow the number plan, though. What's more important is to have a good time and regard Chinese cooking as a pleasure, not a production.

For this reason, contrast in flavor and texture should not be the only consideration when planning a menu. These questions must be asked: Is the time schedule realistic? What can be done in advance? Do I have enough equipment? (If you use a wok for stir-frying, you can't count on it for steaming.) Will a steamer, a pot, and a wok fit on my range at the same time? How can I most easily serve the food—all at once or in sequence —and still eat with my guests?

Family-style Meals

At a family-style meal, the Chinese serve all the food at one time. Their trick is to prepare ahead— chop vegetables, slice and marinate meats, assemble sauces, wash rice, set long-cooking dishes to simmer.

We have eaten superb six-course meals cooked with ease in tiny ovenless kitchens in less than 30 minutes. As each stir-fried or deep-fried dish was completed, it was transferred to a serving bowl and covered with a plate to keep it warm while the next batch of ingredients went into the wok. When the food went to the table the kitchen was in order, for each dish used to hold the uncooked ingredients became the container for serving. This multiple use of space and equipment is inherent in the Chinese way of life.

However, your kitchen is probably larger and more equipped than the typical Chinese kitchen. So, for a multicourse menu, you can plan to prepare something on top of the stove, something in the oven, something that can be done ahead and reheated, something steamed, something that was meant to be served cold, and only one last-minute stir-fried dish.

Banquet-style Meals

If you prefer to serve banquet-style, with each dish coming to the table separately, you may wish to make it an informal meal to facilitate the serving. Have each dish prepared in advance to the point of last-minute cooking or reheating (with a check list to remind yourself of what to do). Guests are willing to wait for each course— and some may even be eager to see just what's going on in the kitchen. Two chefs, or three, don't spoil this type of meal.

Colorful ingredients make beautiful dishes. Use the photograph at right as a guide at the market. From top left: 1. Sesame oil 2. Long grain rice 3. Oyster sauce 4. Soy sauce 5. Chinese tea 6. Rice sticks 7. Szechwan preserved turnip 8. Chili oil 9. Pickled ginger 10. Plum sauce 11. Bean threads 12. Chinese hot mustard 13. Sweet bean sauce 14. Hoisin sauce 15. Bamboo shoots 16. Abalone 17. Bean sauce 18. Kumquats 19. Lychees 20. Pickled mixed vegetables 21. Water chestnuts 22. Hot bean sauce 23. Bean curd 24. Baby corn 25. Quail eggs 26. Oriental eggplant 27. Red snapper 28. Fresh coriander (also called Chinese parsley or cilantro) 29. Snow peas 30. Bok choy 31. Green onions 32. Chinese sausage 33. Chinese cabbage 34. Garlic 35. Fresh ginger 36. Cashew nuts 37. Dried chestnuts 38. Dried chile peppers 39. Star anise 40. Dried mushrooms 41. Fermented black beans 42. Dried shrimp 43. Crushed red pepper 44. Winter melon 45. Dried lily buds 46. Dried black fungus 47. Chinese five-spice 48. Szechwan peppercorns

One of the bonuses of serving dishes individually is that you can take time to savor each bite. For the Chinese, eating is only part of a special meal—one needs time to discuss the food and praise the cook.

Remember, though: no matter how you serve, cook ahead as much as possible. In our recipes we've indicated those that reheat well and those that can be frozen; and keep in mind that any stir-fried dish can be made wok-ready and refrigerated early in the day.

How Much to Serve

While a meal for guests may be the epitome of conspicuous consumption, the Chinese have long known that to eat lightly is to eat well. Yet what is satisfaction for one may be satiety for another. When estimating servings for the recipes in this book, we have considered most dishes that contain meat, poultry, or seafood as a single main course to be served with rice.

So when you plan a Chinese menu that includes several dishes, add up the total number of pounds of boneless meat, poultry, and seafood in all the recipes you plan to cook, then allow a ⅓ pound total of meat, poultry, and seafood for each person.

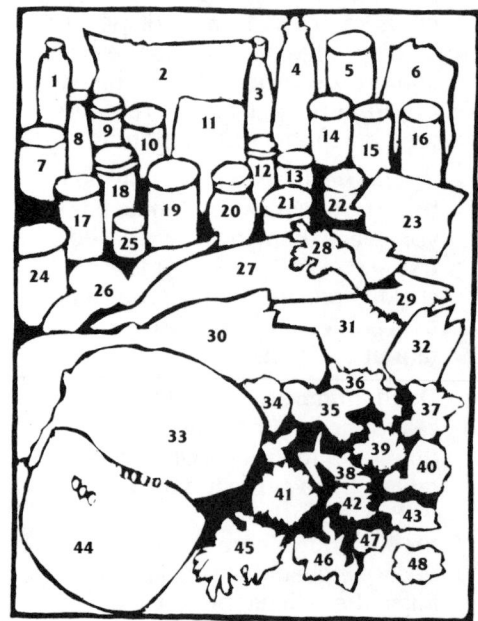

Appetizers

The prelude to a Chinese meal is seldom a drawn-out affair. Unlike the Western custom of setting aside a period of time before dinner for guests to enjoy appetizers with cold drinks away from the table, Chinese hospitality calls for a meal to begin at the table. The seated guests are served small dishes of peanuts or melon seeds for nibbling; or at a big affair, they may be offered a beautifully arranged dish of cold meats, eggs, and marinated vegetables.

The components of this appetizer cold plate are simply prepared and most can be done in advance. They are so good you could serve them in quantity to make a meal. A jug of fruity white wine or sparkling cider is a good match for the variety of robust and delicate flavors.

If your choice is a hot appetizer, you'll find many ideas in this chapter and throughout the book. With the Chinese penchant for serving small dishes, almost any recipe in this book can serve as an appetizer as well as part of a meal. For more ideas, check the listing in the index under "Appetizers."

Chinese Beef Jerky

A favorite Chinese appetizer is jerky—more moist and less brittle than our cowboy jerky. You pre-cook the meat in two stages; this eliminates the extensive drying that most jerky requires.

After this precooking, drying the meat in a moderately hot oven for a short time preserves it enough so you can keep it moist and tender for several months in the refrigerator.

- 3 **pounds lean boneless beef, such as rump or sirloin tip**
- 2 **cups water**
- ⅓ **cup soy sauce**
- 1 **tablespoon dry sherry**
- ¼ **cup sugar**
- 1 **teaspoon salt**
- 2 **whole star anise or 2 teaspoons anise seeds and two 2-inch cinnamon sticks**
- 4 **quarter-size slices fresh ginger, crushed with the side of a cleaver**
- 2 **whole green onions**
- 3 **or 4 small, dry, hot chile peppers**

Cut meat lengthwise into long strips about 3 inches thick and wide. Place in a wide frying pan with the water, soy, sherry, sugar, salt, star anise, ginger, onions, and chile peppers. Bring to a boil, then reduce heat, cover, and simmer, turning meat occasionally, for 30 minutes.

Remove meat from cooking liquid, cool, and chill for at least 1 hour or until firm. Thinly slice meat across the grain. Return meat slices to cooking liquid. Cook, uncovered, over medium heat, turning slices occasionally, until all liquid is absorbed (about 50 minutes). Turn meat more frequently as liquid is absorbed. Discard onions, ginger, and star anise.

Arrange strips of meat slightly apart in a single layer on cooky sheets. Bake, uncovered, in a 300° oven until dry to the touch but still pliable (about 20 minutes). Pat dry any beads of oil with paper towels. Let cool thoroughly. Place in plastic bag, seal, and store in refrigerator up to 2 months. Makes about 1 pound jerky.

Star Anise Tongue

(Pictured on page 18)

The Chinese serve an appetizer cold plate with thin slices of cooked meat the way we serve cold cuts. The slices are cut in bite-size pieces and arranged in neat overlapping layers. This recipe for tongue and the variation with pork are good choices to serve a fairly large group.

    3   pound fresh beef tongue
    3   cups water
    ⅓   cup soy sauce
    3   tablespoons dry sherry
    2   tablespoons sugar
    3   quarter-size slices fresh ginger,
          crushed with the side of a
          cleaver
    2   cloves garlic, minced
    2   whole star anise or 2 teaspoons
          anise seeds and two 2-inch
          cinnamon sticks

Place tongue in a 4-quart or larger pan. Add water, soy, sherry, sugar, ginger, garlic, and star anise. Bring to a boil, then reduce heat and simmer, covered, turning meat occasionally, for 2 hours. Remove tongue and cool slightly; remove and discard skin and any fat, then return meat to pan. Continue simmering, covered, until meat is fork-tender (about 1 more hour). Lift out meat, cool, cover, and chill until cold. Thinly slice meat across the grain; cut large slices in half crosswise. Makes 12 to 16 appetizer servings.

注意 **Star anise pork.** (Pictured on page 18) Follow directions for star anise tongue, but substitute pork for the tongue: a 3-pound piece of boneless pork butt or shoulder or, for neater slices, 2 or 3 pork tenderloins (½ lb. each). Cook pork butt or shoulder for 2½ hours or pork tenderloin for 1 hour or until meat is fork tender.

Barbecued Pork

Canton

Also called *char siu*, barbecued pork is so delicious to eat and can be used so many ways that you may want to keep small portions of it on hand in the freezer. The Chinese serve it as an appetizer, and as a garnish to provide extra flavor for fried rice, won ton soup, noodles, or stir-fried vegetables.

    ¼   cup soy sauce
    2   tablespoons *each* honey, sugar,
          and dry sherry
    1   teaspoon *each* salt and Chinese
          five-spice
    3   quarter-size slices fresh ginger,
          crushed with the side of a
          cleaver
    3   pounds boneless lean pork

In a pan, combine soy, honey, sugar, sherry, salt, five-spice, and ginger. Heat for 1 minute to dissolve sugar; cool.

Cut meat in 1-inch-thick slices and place in a plastic bag. Pour cooled marinade over meat, then seal and refrigerate for 4 hours or until next day. Turn bag occasionally to distribute marinade.

Remove meat from marinade and place on a rack set over a foil-lined baking pan; reserve marinade. Bake in a 350° oven for 30 minutes. Turn pieces over and continue baking for 45 minutes, brushing occasionally with reserved marinade. Cut in thin slices and serve hot or cold. Makes about 2½ pounds barbecued pork.

Drunk Chicken

Shanghai

Because it cooks by steaming, this chicken stays meltingly tender. The longer it marinates in sherry, the more drunk it becomes. Traditionally the meat is left on the bone and hacked into small pieces, but for easier eating, bone the chicken before you marinate it.

    1½ pounds chicken breasts
    2   teaspoons salt
    2   whole green onions
    2   thin slices fresh ginger, crushed
          with the side of a cleaver
    ½   cup dry sherry

Split chicken breasts in half. Rub with salt, cover, and chill for

2 hours. Pour off any liquid that forms, and place chicken in a heatproof bowl that will fit inside a steamer. Cover with onions and ginger. Steam over boiling water for 30 minutes.

Remove from heat and let chicken and cooking juices cool. Pull meat off bones in large pieces and place in a plastic bag with cooking juices and sherry. Seal bag and refrigerate for at least 1 day or as long as 4 days.

Turn bag occasionally to distribute marinade. To serve, remove meat from marinade, cut in bite-size pieces, and arrange on a serving dish. Makes 6 to 8 servings.

Marinated Abalone

Peking

The Chinese are so fond of abalone that menus in Chinese restaurants in the Orient list it as a separate category the way we list dishes made with beef. For an appetizer, nothing could be easier to prepare. You simply slice the chewy, canned abalone and marinate it in a light dressing.

    1   teaspoon sesame seeds
    2   tablespoons *each* white vinegar
          and water
    3   tablespoons soy sauce
    1   teaspoon sugar
    1   whole green onion, thinly sliced
          Dash of ground red pepper
          (cayenne)
    1   can (about 8 oz.) abalone

Place sesame seeds in a small frying pan and cook over medium heat, shaking pan frequently, until seeds begin to pop and turn golden (about 2 minutes). Remove pan from heat and stir in vinegar, water, soy, sugar, green onion, and red pepper.

Drain abalone (save the liquid for soup) and thinly slice. Place in a plastic bag, pour marinade over abalone slices, and seal. Chill for at least 2 hours, turning bag occasionally to distribute marinade. To serve, drain and arrange on a serving dish. Makes 6 to 8 servings.

Glazed Spareribs

Since these are easiest to eat with fingers, you might want to serve this appetizer at an outdoor meal or picnic and provide small damp cloths—the Chinese call them fragrant towels—for wiping hands.

- ½ side (1½ lbs.) pork spareribs
- 3 tablespoons soy sauce
- 1 tablespoon dry sherry
- 1 teaspoon sugar
- 1 tablespoon cornstarch
- 1 clove garlic, minced
  Glazing sauce (directions follow)
  Salad oil

Have your meatman cut spareribs through the bones crosswise to make about 1½-inch lengths. Cut bones apart, leaving an equal amount of meat on each section. In a bowl, blend soy, sherry, sugar, cornstarch, and garlic. Add meat and stir to coat. Let stand for 30 minutes to marinate.

Prepare glazing sauce and reserve.

In a deep pan, pour salad oil to a depth of 2 inches and heat to 360° on a deep-frying thermometer. Add about one-fourth of the meat at a time to the hot oil and cook until meat is no longer pink in the middle and is well browned outside (about 8 minutes). Remove with a slotted spoon and drain on paper towels. Drop cooked spareribs into glazing sauce and mix well. Serve at room temperature or, if made ahead, cover and reheat in a 350° oven for 15 minutes. Makes 6 to 8 servings.

Glazing sauce. In a pan, blend 1 tablespoon *each* **dry sherry, vinegar,** and **soy sauce;** 2 tablespoons **sugar;** and 1 teaspoon **cornstarch.** Cook, stirring, until slightly thickened.

Appetizer cold plate offers a contrast of flavors and textures. Clockwise from top left: Sesame Eggplant Salad (page 77), Star Anise Tongue (page 17), canned quail eggs, Cold-stirred Lima Beans (page 74), Vegetable Pickles (page 76), Star Anise Pork (page 17), White Cut Chicken with Spicy Peanut Sauce (page 48).

Pork-stuffed Clams

Small clam shells make neat serving containers for this alloy of pork and clams. The easiest way to serve this as an appetizer is to place 3 or 4 shells on each small serving plate and provide small forks.

- 2 pounds small clams in the shell
- 1 cup water
- ½ pound boneless lean pork, finely chopped or ground
- ¼ cup water chestnuts, finely chopped
- 1 whole green onion, minced
- 1 tablespoon *each* soy sauce, dry sherry, and cornstarch
- ½ teaspoon *each* salt and minced fresh ginger
- 1 teaspoon sugar
  Dash of white pepper

Scrub clams well with a brush. Place in a wide frying pan and add water. Bring to a boil, then cover and simmer until all the shells open (about 5 minutes). Cool; drain off broth and save for soup. Remove clams from shells; finely chop clam meat. Separate each shell to make two halves; turn upside down to drain. Combine clams with pork, water chestnuts, onion, soy, sherry, cornstarch, salt, ginger, sugar, and pepper; mix well.

Mound about 4 teaspoons clam-pork mixture inside of each shell. Arrange shells, filled side up, on heatproof plates that will fit inside a steamer. If made ahead, cover and refrigerate for as long as 8 hours, but bring to room temperature before steaming.

To cook, place plate on a rack in steamer, cover, and steam over boiling water for 20 minutes or until pork is cooked throughout. Serve the first portion while you steam the second. Makes about 20 filled shells.

Spiced Chicken Livers

Shanghai

No style of Chinese cooking is easier to execute than red cooking —braising food in liquid seasoned with soy sauce. These chicken livers turn a rich mahogany color and develop a spicy flavor.

- 1 pound chicken livers
- ½ cup *each* soy sauce and water
- ¼ cup dry sherry
- 1 tablespoon sugar
- ½ star anise or ½ teaspoon anise seed and 1 1-inch cinnamon stick
- 1 quarter-size slice fresh ginger, crushed with the side of a cleaver
- 1 whole green onion, cut in 1-inch lengths
- ¼ teaspoon crushed red pepper (optional)

Place livers in a pan, cover with water, and bring just to boiling; drain. Add soy, the ½ cup water, sherry, sugar, star anise, ginger, onion, and red pepper (if used). Bring just to boiling, cover, and simmer for 15 minutes. Remove from heat and cool. Slice livers in bite-size pieces, return to stock, and chill for at least 1 hour or as long as 2 days. To serve, drain, discard ginger and green onion, and arrange on a serving dish. Makes 6 to 8 servings.

Curry Beef Pockets

Canton

You can make these savory appetizers with ready-to-fill wrappers—egg roll skins, similar to won ton skins but larger. The skins vary in size from 6 inches square to 8 inches square, but any dimension in this range will work. You cut each skin in thirds and fold the strips to form triangles, the same way you fold a flag.

- ½ pound lean ground beef
- ½ small onion, finely chopped
- 2 teaspoons curry powder
- ¼ teaspoon salt
- 1½ teaspoons *each* soy sauce and dry sherry
- 16 egg roll skins
- 1 egg
  Salad oil
  Hot mustard (page 37) or catsup

(Continued on next page)

In a wide frying pan over medium-high heat, cook beef and onion until meat is brown and crumbly and onion is tender. Stir in curry powder, salt, soy, and sherry, and cook for 1 minute; cool.

Cut each skin in three equal strips. Beat egg lightly. To fill and fold pockets, see illustration below. **1.** Fold bottom corner of a strip to form a triangle. Fold triangle over again on itself. **2.** In the pocket formed, place about 1 teaspoon filling. **3.** Continue folding triangle over until the entire length of the strip is folded. Seal final fold with beaten egg. Repeat until all the strips are filled.

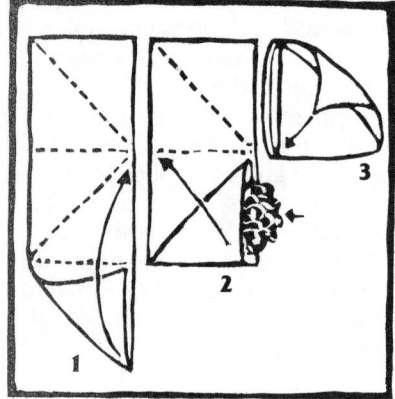

Place filled pockets slightly apart on a baking sheet and cover while you fill the remaining strips. At this point you can cover and refrigerate up to 8 hours, but bring to room temperature before cooking.

In a deep pan (at least 6 inches in diameter), pour salad oil to a depth of 1½ inches and heat to 350° on a deep-frying thermometer. Fry 4 to 6 pockets at a time, turning occasionally, for 2 minutes or until golden brown. Remove with a slotted spoon and drain on paper towels. Keep warm in a 200° oven until all are cooked, then serve with a dipping sauce of hot mustard or catsup. If cooked ahead, cool pockets, then freeze in plastic bags. To reheat, arrange in a single layer on a baking sheet (while still frozen) and heat in a 350° oven for 12 to 15 minutes. Makes 4 dozen appetizers.

Paper-wrapped Chicken

Canton

Good food comes in small packages when you wrap it the Chinese way. You place morsels of marinated chicken, seafood, or meat on cooking parchment squares, fold them into tiny envelopes, and cook the packets immediately before serving. To eat, you open the wrapping with your fingers and pick up each bite with chopsticks or a fork.

Cooking parchment is an opaque sturdy paper made for cooking. It is sold in rolls, like wax paper, and can be found in the paper products section of most markets.

Traditionally the packets are fried in deep fat. We also give directions for a lighter version which you bake in the oven. And you can wrap the packets as much as 6 hours in advance of cooking time.

1 tablespoon *each* soy sauce, dry sherry, and hoisin sauce
1 teaspoon *each* cornstarch and salad oil
½ teaspoon *each* sesame oil and sugar
  Dash of pepper
1 pound chicken breasts, skinned, boned, and cut in bite-size pieces
2 ounces cooked ham or Chinese sausages
5 whole green onions
30 leaves fresh coriander (also called Chinese parsley or cilantro)
  Salad oil (optional)

In a bowl, combine soy, sherry, hoisin sauce, cornstarch, the 1 teaspoon salad oil, sesame oil, sugar, and pepper. Add chicken and marinate for 30 minutes.

Cut ham, if used, in matchstick pieces. If you use Chinese sausages instead, steam them on a rack over boiling water for 15 minutes, then cut diagonally in slices ⅛ inch thick; you should have 30 slices. Cut green onions in 1½-inch lengths, then slice lengthwise in thin shreds. Cut

cooking parchment into 30 5-inch squares.

To wrap chicken, see illustration below .**1.** In center of each parchment square, place 1 piece chicken, 3 strips ham (or 1 slice Chinese sausage), several shreds of green onion, and a leaf of coriander. Turn one corner up over filling. **2.** Fold adjacent corners in toward center, overlapping and enclosing filling. **3.** Fold filled part of packet in half (see dotted line). **4.** Slide fourth corner all the way down into space between layers of paper to seal each packet. At this point you can cover and refrigerate up to 6 hours until ready to cook.

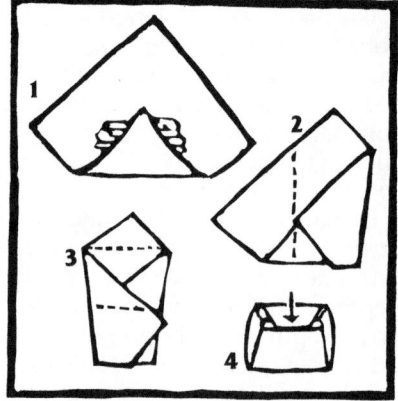

In a deep pan (at least 6 inches in diameter), pour salad oil to a depth of 1½ inches and heat to 350° on a deep-frying thermometer. Fry 4 to 6 packets at a time, turning occasionally, for 3 minutes or until chicken is opaque. Remove with a slotted spoon and drain on paper towels. Keep warm in a 200° oven until all are cooked.

Or arrange packets in a single layer in a shallow, rimmed baking pan. Bake in a 400° oven for 12 minutes. Makes 30.

注意 **Paper-wrapped scallops.** Cut ½ pound **scallops** in ¼-inch-thick slices. In a bowl, combine 2 tablespoons **dry sherry**, ½ teaspoon *each* **salt** and minced fresh **ginger**, 1 clove **garlic** (minced), 1 teaspoon **cornstarch**, 2 teaspoons **salad oil**, and ¼ teaspoon **sesame oil**. Add scallops and marinate for 30 minutes.

Cover 6 medium-size **dried mushrooms** with **warm water,** let stand for 30 minutes, then drain. Cut off and discard stems; squeeze mushrooms dry and thinly slice. Cut 2 ounces **cooked ham** in matchstick pieces. Cut 4 whole **green onions** in 1½-inch lengths, then slice lengthwise in thin shreds. Cut cooking parchment into 24 5-inch squares.

To wrap scallops, follow directions for paper-wrapped chicken, but fill each packet with 1 scallop slice and several strips of mushroom, ham, and onion. Cook in deep fat (350°) for 2 minutes or bake in a 400° oven for 10 minutes or until scallops are opaque. Makes 24.

注意 **Paper-wrapped pork.** Cut a **pork tenderloin** (about ½ lb.) crosswise in ¼-inch-thick slices. In a bowl, combine 1 teaspoon *each* **cornstarch** and **sugar;** 1 tablespoon *each* **dry sherry, hoisin sauce,** and **salad oil;** ¼ teaspoon **sesame oil;** a dash of **pepper;** and 3 drops **liquid hot pepper seasoning.** Add pork and marinate for 30 minutes. Cover 6 medium-size **dried mushrooms** with **warm water,** let stand for 30 minutes, then drain. Cut off and discard stems; squeeze mushrooms dry and thinly slice. Cut 4 whole **green onions** in 1½-inch lengths, then slice lengthwise in thin shreds. Cut cooking parchment into 24 5-inch squares.

To wrap pork, follow directions for paper-wrapped chicken, filling each packet with 1 slice meat and several strips of mushroom and green onion. Cook in deep fat (350°) for 5 minutes or bake in a 400° oven for 14 minutes or until pork is cooked through. Makes 24.

Egg Rolls

(Pictured on page 50)

The Canton region calls this fried pastry "egg roll." In Shanghai, the name is "spring roll." The type of wrapper used to encase the savory filling determines the name. Egg

roll wrapper skins make a coating with considerable substance while the thin spring roll skins give a more delicate crust.

The wrappers are available in 1-pound packages in Chinese markets and in the refrigerator and freezer sections of many supermarkets. The two can be used interchangeably, but it takes tremendous patience to separate spring roll skins which have been frozen, and if you wish to use a thin wrapper it is as easy to make your own.

The Chinese cut egg rolls in sections to serve and that is the best way to present them as appetizers. For snacks they'll disappear quickly, so leave them whole.

> **Crab or ham filling (directions follow)**
> **Sweet and sour sauce (directions follow)**
> 1 **package (1 lb.) egg roll or spring roll skins or freshly prepared spring roll skins (directions follow)**
> 1 **egg, lightly beaten**
> **Salad oil**
> **Soy sauce (optional)**

Prepare crab or ham filling and cool. Prepare sweet and sour sauce and cool. To fill and wrap egg rolls, follow the directions below. **1.** Mound about 2 rounded tablespoons cooled filling across each egg roll skin in a 3-inch strip, about 2 inches above the lower corner. Fold bottom corner over filling to cover, then roll over once to enclose filling. **2.** Fold over left and right corners, then brush sides

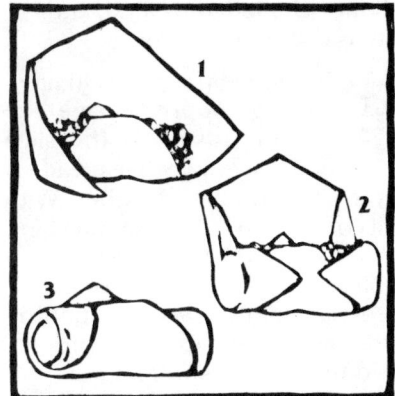

and top of triangle with beaten egg. **3.** Roll, sealing corner. Place filled egg rolls on a baking sheet and cover while you fill the remaining skins. At this point you can cover and refrigerate up to 8 hours.

In a deep pan, pour salad oil to a depth of 1½ inches and heat to 360° on a deep-frying thermometer. Fry 3 or 4 egg rolls at a time, turning as needed, until golden brown (about 2 to 3 minutes). Remove with a slotted spoon and drain on paper towels. Keep warm in a 200° oven until all are cooked. Serve with sweet and sour sauce or soy sauce, if desired.

If cooked ahead, cool egg rolls, then refrigerate or freeze in plastic bags. To reheat, place rolls (do not thaw if frozen) in a single layer in a shallow-rimmed pan; bake, uncovered, in a 350° oven for 15 minutes (25 minutes if frozen) or until hot. Makes about 2 dozen.

Crab filling. Prepare the following: ½ teaspoon minced fresh **ginger;** ¾ pound **bean sprouts;** ¾ cup chopped fresh **mushrooms;** 1 cup thinly sliced **celery;** ¾ cup chopped **bamboo shoots;** ¾ pound cooked or canned **crab meat** flaked, then squeezed to eliminate excess liquid; and 2 whole **green onions,** thinly sliced. In a bowl, combine 1½ teaspoons *each* **dry sherry** and **soy sauce,** ½ teaspoon *each* **sugar** and **salt,** and 1 teaspoon *each* **cornstarch** and **sesame oil.**

Heat a wok or wide frying pan over high heat. When pan is hot, add 2 tablespoons **salad oil.** When oil begins to heat, add ginger. Stir once, then add bean sprouts, mushrooms, celery, and bamboo shoots. Stir-fry for 2 minutes. Add crab and green onion; stir sherry-soy mixture, add to pan, and cook, stirring, until pan juices thicken. Cool.

Ham filling. Prepare the following: 1 clove **garlic,** minced; ½ teaspoon grated fresh **ginger;** 1 large **onion,** chopped; 1 cup thinly sliced **celery;** 1 pound cooked **ham,** cut in matchstick pieces; ½ cup sliced **bamboo shoots,** cut in matchstick pieces; and 2 cups finely shredded **cabbage.**

Combine 1 tablespoon **cornstarch,** ½ teaspoon **salt,** 2 teaspoons **soy sauce,** and 1 tablespoon **dry sherry;** set aside.

Heat a wok or wide frying pan over high heat. When pan is hot, add 2 tablespoons **salad oil.** When oil begins to heat, add garlic and ginger. Stir once, then add onion and celery and stir-fry for 1 minute. Add ham, bamboo shoots, and cabbage; stir-fry for about 2 minutes. Stir cornstarch mixture once, add to pan, and cook, stirring, until sauce bubbles and thickens. Cool.

Sweet and sour sauce. In a pan combine 1 tablespoon **cornstarch,** 3 tablespoons *each* **sugar** and **wine vinegar,** 1 tablespoon *each* **soy sauce** and tomato-based **chili sauce,** dash of **ground red pepper** (cayenne), and ½ cup **chicken broth.** Cook, stirring, until thickened. Cool.

Spring roll skins. Mix together 1 cup unsifted **all-purpose flour** and 1 cup plus 2 tablespoons **water** until smooth. Let stand 15 minutes.

Heat a wide frying pan or griddle with a nonstick finish over medium heat. Using a wide pastry brush or new wide paint brush, brush on a thin layer of batter in approximately a 6-inch square. If holes appear, brush over some more batter in the opposite direction. As soon as batter appears dry and edges begin to curl (about 15 seconds), lift wrapper from pan and cool (do not stack). Repeat until all batter is used. Fill at once, or separate with pieces of wax paper, cover tightly, and refrigerate for as long as 1 day. Makes about 2 dozen spring roll skins.

Shrimp Toast

Peking   (Pictured on opposite page)

Every region of China makes its local variation of this savory hot appetizer. In this version, you cut the bread in finger-length strips instead of squares, then dip the toast in a salt-pepper mix before eating. If you don't have day-old bread, leave the slices on a rack for several hours to dry slightly before covering with the shrimp mixture. Very fresh bread soaks up too much oil during deep frying.

> 6 **sandwich-size slices firm, day-old white bread**
> **Shrimp filling (directions follow)**
> 1½ **teaspoons sesame seeds**
> **Salt-pepper mix (page 37)**

Remove crusts from bread. Spread about 1 tablespoon filling on each slice, pressing it firmly to bread and rounding the corners. Sprinkle ¼ teaspoon sesame seeds over filling on each slice. If made ahead, arrange in a single layer in a baking pan, cover, and chill up to 8 hours.

In a deep pan (at least 6 inches in diameter), pour salad oil to a depth of 1½ inches and heat to 350° on a deep-frying thermometer. Fry slices, shrimp side down, for 1 minute. Turn over and continue cooking until shrimp filling is cooked through (about 1 minute). Remove and drain on paper towels. Keep warm in a 200° oven until all are cooked. Cut each slice crosswise in 4 fingers and serve hot with salt-pepper mix for dipping. Makes 24.

Shrimp filling. In a bowl, beat 1 **egg white** until foamy. Blend 2 teaspoons *each* **dry sherry** and **cornstarch,** then stir into egg white along with ½ teaspoon *each* **salt** and grated fresh **ginger.** Add ¼ cup **water chestnuts** (finely chopped) and ½ pound medium-size **raw shrimp** (shelled, deveined, and finely chopped); mix well.

注意 **Diamond shrimp balls.** (Pictured on opposite page) Remove crusts from 6 thin slices firm, day-old, **white bread.** Cut each slice into ¼-inch cubes. With oil coated hands, roll **shrimp filling** above into 16 walnut-size balls. Roll each ball in cubes of bread, pressing gently as you roll, until all sides are coated. Cook according to directions for shrimp toast. Serve hot with salt-pepper mix (page 37) for dipping. Makes 16.

Crab Pillows

(Pictured on opposite page)

Meant to be eaten with chopsticks but just as easily picked up with fingers, these tiny open-faced sandwiches make a delicious hot appetizer to pass at a party. You assemble them ahead, then deep fry them just before serving.

> 1 **egg white**
> 1 **teaspoon** *each* **water and dry sherry**
> 2 **teaspoons cornstarch**
> ½ **teaspoon salt**
> 1 **teaspoon grated fresh ginger**
> 2 **tablespoons chopped fresh coriander (also called Chinese parsley or cilantro)**
> 1 **cup cooked or canned crab, flaked**
> 6 **sandwich-size slices firm, day-old white bread**
> **Salad oil**

In a bowl, beat together egg white, water, and sherry until foamy. Stir in cornstarch, salt, ginger, and coriander. Squeeze crab lightly to eliminate any moisture, then stir into egg white mixture.

Remove crusts from bread; cut each slice in 4 squares. Mound about 2 teaspoons of crab mixture on each square, pressing it firmly to bread and rounding the corners. If made ahead, arrange in a single layer in a baking pan, cover, and chill up to 8 hours.

In a deep pan (at least 6 inches in diameter), pour salad oil to a depth of 1½ inches and heat to 350° on a deep-frying thermometer. Fry 4 squares at a time, crab side down, until the edges begin to brown (about 30 seconds).

Turn over and fry for 10 seconds longer; remove and drain on paper towels. Serve immediately. Makes 24.

Hot and cold Chinese appetizers make great party food. Clockwise from top center: Ginger Beef (page 41); Diamond Shrimp Balls, Shrimp Toast, and Crab Pillows (page 22); Fried Won Ton (page 87); Chicken Wings with Sweet & Pungent Sauce (page 48); Marinated Lotus Root, Carrots, and Snow Peas (page 77).

Soups

The Chinese don't consider soup a separate course. At a family meal, soup always goes to the table to act as a beverage. At a banquet, two or three soups may appear as a welcome pause between rich, spicy dishes.

Most Chinese soups are light and fast to prepare. You simply embellish stock with a bowlful of fresh vegetables or bits of meat. There are notable exceptions, however. Shark's fin and bird's nest soups are time consuming and costly to prepare. You might want to try these festive dishes in a restaurant.

For Western meals, the lighter soups make a fine beginning, offering heart-warming flavor but few calories. If you serve a Chinese meal, soup is a pleasant way to set the stage and allow you time to assemble the next dish.

Chicken Broth

Chicken broth is important in Chinese cooking because it gives smoothness and a depth of flavor to soups and cooking sauces. Canned broth is fine to use when you are in a hurry. The great advantage of making your own is that you can make it without salt. Since many seasonings called for in Chinese cooking are naturally salty, you don't need to worry about excessive saltiness if you cook with homemade broth.

When you cut up poultry (or pork) for stir-frying, save the bones to convert into broth. (The Chinese generally consider broth made from beef bones too overpowering in flavor.)

Our recipe is for a light stock which makes a good starting point for soups. Use it alone or use it to enrich and extend canned broth without increasing the salt content. If you have not quite mastered the technique of boning and find that you don't remove every bit of meat, take heart—your soup broth will have an even richer flavor.

3 **pounds bony chicken pieces (necks, backs, wings, or any other uncooked bones), or uncooked pork bones and trimmings, or a combination of both**
2 **quarts water**
2 **quarter-size slices fresh ginger, crushed with the side of a cleaver**
2 **whole green onions, cut in half**
 Salt

Combine chicken pieces, water, ginger, and onions in a large pan and bring to a boil. Skim off any foam that rises to the top. Cover and simmer for 2 hours. Pour broth through a colander; discard residue. Cool and chill. When broth is cool, spoon off fat and discard, if you wish. Chinese cooks prefer to leave a little fat to give a smooth texture to the broth. Refrigerate up to 3 days or freeze for longer storage. Add salt to taste when you use the broth. Makes about 1½ quarts.

Duck Soup

Peking   (Pictured on page 31)

At a traditional Peking duck dinner, the duck stars in three roles—as crisp skin, succulent meat, and delicate soup. Restaurants can offer this presentation because they make the soup from a back-up duck. At home, it is easier to serve the soup at another meal. After slicing the meat from Peking-style ducks or plain roast chickens, refrigerate or freeze the bones to make this elegant soup. If you use the carcasses from two birds, the soup will develop an even richer flavor.

The lotus seeds or ginkgo nuts used in the soup have a texture similar to chestnuts and are good in many different soups. Both are sold canned. After opening, transfer to a jar and cover with cold water. Refrigerate up to a week, but change the water frequently.

> **Bones from 1 or 2 Peking-style ducks (page 52), or plain roast chickens, or a combination of both**
> 1 **stalk celery, cut in 1-inch lengths**
> 1 **whole green onion, cut in half**
> 1 **thin slice fresh ginger, crushed with the side of a cleaver**
> 5 **cups water**
> 6 **medium-size dried mushrooms**
> 1 **teaspoon dry sherry**
> ½ **teaspoon cornstarch**
> ½ **pound chicken breasts, skinned, boned, and cut in bite-size pieces**
> ⅓ **cup dried or canned lotus seeds or canned ginkgo nuts**
> ½ **cup water chestnuts, sliced**
> ½ **cup sliced bamboo shoots**
> 2 **teaspoons soy sauce**
> 1 **whole green onion, thinly sliced**
> **Salt**

Combine duck bones, celery, onion, ginger, and water in a large pan and bring to a boil. Skim off any foam that rises to the top. Cover and simmer for 2 hours. Pour broth through a colander; discard residue. Cool and chill long enough for fat to come to the top. Discard fat. You should have 4 cups broth. If not, add chicken broth or water to make up the difference.

Cover mushrooms with warm water, let stand for 30 minutes, then drain. Cut off and discard stems; squeeze mushrooms dry and thinly slice. In a bowl, blend sherry and cornstarch; add chicken and stir to coat. If you use dried lotus seeds, cover with warm water, let stand for 30 minutes, then drain. Simmer in water to cover for 30 minutes, then drain.

In a 2-quart pan, heat broth just to boiling. Add mushrooms, water chestnuts, bamboo shoots, lotus seeds or ginkgo nuts, and soy. Cover and simmer for 20 minutes. Add chicken, stir several times, and continue to simmer for 10 minutes. Stir in sliced onion and season with salt to taste just before serving. Makes 4 to 6 servings.

Shrimp Ball Soup

Peking   (Pictured on page 26)

Fluffy shrimp balls, silky bean threads, and crisp snow peas provide an interesting contrast of textures in this soup. You can prepare the shrimp balls in advance, so the soup is quick to assemble.

> **Shrimp filling (page 22)**
> 2 **ounces bean threads**
> 4 **cups chicken broth, page 24 or canned**
> 1 **teaspoon *each* dry sherry and soy sauce**
> ¼ **pound mushrooms, thinly sliced**
> 20 **snow peas, ends and strings removed**
> 3 **sprigs fresh coriander (also called Chinese parsley or cilantro)**
> **Salt**

With oil-coated hands, roll shrimp filling into walnut-size balls. Heat a pan of water to simmering. Drop in shrimp balls a few at a time and simmer gently until they float (about 4 to 5 minutes). Drain and discard liquid. If made ahead, cool, cover, and refrigerate up to two days.

Cover bean threads with warm water and let stand for 30 minutes. Drain, then place on a cutting board and cut in 6-inch lengths.

In a 2-quart pan heat chicken broth, sherry, and soy just to boiling. Add bean threads and mushrooms and simmer, uncovered, for 5 minutes. Add snow peas and cook for 2 minutes. Add shrimp balls and cook just until heated through. Garnish with coriander and season to taste with salt. Makes 4 to 6 servings.

Shrimp with Tomato Soup

Shanghai   (Pictured on page 26)

Garnished with egg slivers, this soup is refreshing and light. If you wish to make a heartier version, use bean curd in place of the egg.

> ¼ **pound medium-size raw shrimp, shelled and deveined**
> 1 **tablespoon dry sherry**
> ½ **small cucumber**
> 2 **tablespoons salad oil**
> 2 **medium-size tomatoes, peeled, seeded, and coarsely chopped**
> 5 **cups chicken broth, page 24 or canned**
> ¼ **pound bean curd or tofu, drained and cut in 1-inch cubes (optional)**
> **Salt and white pepper**
> **Egg slivers (directions follow)**

Marinate shrimp in sherry for 10 minutes. Peel cucumber, leaving alternating strips of green for color. Cut in half lengthwise and scoop out seeds; cut crosswise in ¼-inch-thick slices.

In a 2-quart pan, heat oil over medium heat. Add tomato and stir-fry for 2 minutes. Pour in broth and bring to a boil. Add shrimp, cucumber, and bean curd (if used); simmer, uncovered, for 3 minutes. Just before serving, season to taste with salt and pepper. If you do not use bean curd, garnish with egg slivers. Makes 4 to 6 servings.

Egg slivers. Beat 2 **eggs** with 2 teaspoons **water** and ⅛ teaspoon **salt.** Heat 2 teaspoons **salad oil** in a wide frying pan over medium heat. Pour in egg and tilt pan to

distribute evenly. Cook until egg is still moist but set. Turn out onto board and cool. Roll loosely, then cut into slivers.

Four Delight Sizzling Rice Soup

This soup makes a showy presentation. At the table you slide fried rice cakes into the soup to create a crackling, sizzling sound. Actually, you can add rice cakes to almost any soup in this chapter and give the soup a sizzling name. The trick is to be sure that both rice cakes and soup are piping hot.

- 2 teaspoons *each* soy sauce, dry sherry, and cornstarch
- ⅓ pound boneless lean pork, cut in matchstick pieces
- 4 cups chicken broth, page 24 or canned
- 1 cup sliced fresh mushrooms
- ⅓ cup *each* sliced water chestnuts and frozen green peas (thawed)
- 2 whole green onions, thinly sliced Salt
- 1 teaspoon sesame oil
- 4 2-inch squares sizzling rice (page 81) Salad oil

In a bowl, blend soy, sherry, and cornstarch. Add pork and mix until well coated. Let stand for 10 minutes.

In a 2-quart pan, heat chicken broth to boiling. Add pork, stir several times, then reduce heat and simmer for 5 minutes. Add mushrooms, water chestnuts, and peas. Simmer, uncovered, for 2 minutes. Add green onion, salt to taste, and sesame oil.

Keep soup hot while you fry sizzling rice cakes as directed on page 81. Pour hot soup into a warm tureen and carry to the table. Bring hot fried rice cakes to the table in a bowl and immediately slide into the soup. Makes 4 to 6 servings.

Start a meal with a regional soup. Clockwise from foreground: Shrimp with Tomato Soup (page 25), Hot & Sour Soup (page 27), Shrimp Ball Soup (page 25), Abalone & Mustard Green Soup (page 28).

Pork & Preserved Turnip Soup

Szechwan

The preserved turnip used in this recipe is favored in Szechwan cooking for its sour-spicy-hot flavor. It is sometimes labeled Szechwan preserved mustard. You'll also find it in the recipe for Szechwan-style dry-fried beans (page 73). Though most often used as a cooking ingredient, it can also be thinly sliced and eaten the way you would eat a pickled hot pepper. The gnarled vegetable is sold in small flat cans or plastic bags. After opening, transfer to a jar and refrigerate for as long as six months.

- 6 medium-size dried mushrooms
- 2 teaspoons *each* soy sauce, dry sherry, and cornstarch
- ½ pound boneless lean pork, cut in matchstick pieces
- 1 piece (about ¼ cup) Szechwan preserved turnip
- 6 cups chicken broth, page 24 or canned
- ½ cup sliced bamboo shoots, cut in matchstick pieces
- ½ teaspoon Szechwan hot bean sauce or 1 small, dry hot chile pepper, crumbled and seeded, if desired
- 2 whole green onions, thinly sliced
- 2 cups coarsely sliced spinach leaves
- 1 tablespoon soy sauce Salt

Cover mushrooms with warm water, let stand for 30 minutes, then drain. Cut off and discard stems; squeeze mushrooms dry and thinly slice. In a bowl, blend the 2 teaspoons soy, sherry, and cornstarch. Add pork and mix until well coated. Let stand for 10 minutes. Rinse turnip to eliminate red pickling spice. Cut in matchstick pieces; you should have ¼ cup.

In a 3-quart pan, heat chicken broth to boiling. Add pork, mushrooms, preserved turnip, bamboo shoots, and hot bean sauce. Stir several times, then reduce heat and simmer, uncovered, for 5 minutes. Stir in onion, spinach, and the 1 tablespoon soy and cook for 1 minute. Season with salt to taste. Makes 6 servings.

Hot & Sour Soup

Szechwan (Pictured on page 26)

The meat and vegetables used in this soup vary from kitchen to kitchen—and you can substitute freely—but the use of pepper for the hot flavor, vinegar for the sour taste, as well as egg, are traditional.

- 4 medium-size dried mushrooms or 4 dried black fungus
- ¼ pound boneless lean pork, cut in matchstick pieces
- 1 tablespoon dry sherry
- 4 cups chicken broth, page 24 or canned
- ½ pound chicken breasts, skinned, boned, and cut in matchstick pieces
- ½ cup sliced bamboo shoots, cut in matchstick pieces
- ¼ pound bean curd or tofu, drained and cut in ½-inch cubes
- 2 tablespoons white wine vinegar
- 1 tablespoon soy sauce
- 2 tablespoons cornstarch
- ¼ cup water
- ½ to ¾ teaspoon white pepper
- 1 teaspoon sesame oil
- 1 egg, lightly beaten
- 2 whole green onions, cut in 1-inch diagonal slices Salt

Cover mushrooms with warm water, let stand for 30 minutes, then drain. Cut off and discard stems; squeeze mushrooms dry and thinly slice. If you use fungus, cover with warm water, let stand for 30 minutes, then drain. Pinch out hard knob from center of fungus and discard; cut fungus in thin strips. Combine pork with sherry; let stand for 10 minutes.

In a 2-quart pan, heat chicken broth to boiling. Add mushrooms or fungus, pork, chicken, and bamboo shoots. Stir several times, then reduce heat; cover and simmer 5 minutes. Add bean curd, wine vinegar, and soy; heat, uncovered, for 1 minute. Blend cornstarch and water. Add to soup and cook, stirring, until slightly thickened. Turn off heat. Add pepper and sesame oil. Stirring continuously, slowly pour egg into soup. Sprinkle with onion and salt to taste. Makes 6 servings.

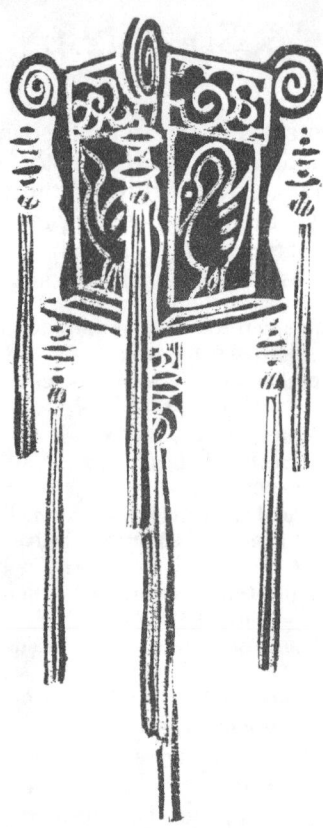

Egg Drop Soup

(Pictured on page 39)

This simple soup derives its name from stirring beaten eggs into chicken broth. On hitting the hot liquid, the eggs cook and form long threads. You can assemble the ingredients ahead of time, but cook the soup at the last minute so the watercress remains green.

- 1 large bunch watercress or 2 cups coarsely sliced spinach leaves
- 4 cups chicken broth, page 24 or canned
- 2 teaspoons *each* dry sherry and soy sauce
- 2 eggs
  Salt

Wash watercress and discard thick stems; break long sprigs in half. In a 2-quart pan heat chicken broth, sherry, and soy to boiling. Add watercress or spinach and simmer, uncovered, for 2 minutes. Beat eggs lightly. Remove pan from heat. Add eggs slowly to soup, stirring constantly, until they form long threads. Season with salt to taste. Makes 4 to 6 servings.

Beef with Shining Noodles Soup

Hunan

Before they are cooked, bean threads look like stiff nylon fishing line. If you start with a large package, use kitchen scissors to cut off the right amount of the tough wiry strands. As they cook, the bean threads become silky and absorb the hot spices. The chiles in this soup are added whole and you can leave them in or remove them as you ladle the soup into a tureen.

- 4 ounces dried bean threads
- 2 teaspoons *each* cornstarch, dry sherry, and salad oil
- ¾ pound boneless lean beef, cut in matchstick pieces
- 3 tablespoons fermented black beans
- 2 tablespoons salad oil
- 1 tablespoon minced garlic
- 3 to 6 small, dry hot chile peppers
- 6 cups chicken broth, page 24 or canned
- 1 tablespoon soy sauce
- 1½ teaspoons sugar
- 3 whole green onions, cut in 2-inch lengths
- 1 teaspoon sesame oil
  Salt

Cover bean threads with warm water and let stand for 30 minutes. Drain, then place on a cutting board and cut in 6-inch lengths. In a bowl, blend cornstarch, sherry, and the 2 teaspoons oil. Add meat and mix well; let stand for 10 minutes. Rinse black beans and drain.

In a 3-quart pan, heat the 2 tablespoons oil over medium heat. Add black beans, garlic, and whole chile peppers. Cook, stirring, until spices smell fragrant and begin to brown (about 1 to 2 minutes). Do not allow spices to burn. Add chicken broth, soy, sugar, and bean threads. Bring to a boil, then reduce heat and simmer, uncovered, for 5 minutes. Stir in meat and onions and cook, stirring occasionally, just until meat loses its pinkness (about 3 minutes). Just before serving, stir in sesame oil and season with salt to taste. Makes 6 servings.

Chicken & Corn Soup

Canton

Many foods not native to China were introduced to the country through the Canton region by 17th century traders. Corn is one example of a "foreign" food which was woven into the local cuisine and cooked Chinese-style.

- 2 egg whites
- ¾ pound chicken breasts, boned, skinned, and finely chopped
- 1 can (about 1 lb.) cream-style corn
- 4 cups chicken broth, page 24 or canned
- 1 teaspoon soy sauce
  Salt
- 2 tablespoons cornstarch
- 3 tablespoons water
  About ¼ cup finely chopped, cooked ham

Beat egg whites until moist peaks form; fold in chopped chicken and reserve. Whirl 1 cup of the corn and 1 cup of the broth in a blender. Combine in a 2-quart pan with the remaining corn and broth. Add soy and salt to taste. Heat slowly. Blend cornstarch and water. Add to soup and cook, stirring, until very slightly thickened. Add chicken-egg white mixture and blend well. Cook on medium heat for 4 minutes, but do not boil. If made ahead, reheat over low heat. Pour into a hot tureen and sprinkle with chopped ham. Makes 4 to 6 servings.

Abalone & Mustard Green Soup

Canton   (Pictured on page 26)

The Chinese consider this a special soup—one to serve at a festive meal. The abalone goes in only at the last minute; longer cooking would make it tough. If you cannot buy a small can of abalone, buy a 1-pound-size can and marinate the remainder to serve as an appetizer (page 17).

(Continued on page 30)

Chinese hot pot dinner

Peking

If you're looking for an easy, festive, and leisurely way to entertain Chinese-style, try cooking a hot pot dinner at the table. The idea originated in Northern China where it was customary to heat rooms in cold weather by burning a little charcoal in a small pot. To double the usefulness of this heat, it was common for a family to set a pot of broth over it and cook small pieces of food.

Today, translated into our Western style of entertaining, the basic plan is simple. You set a selection of meat, seafood, vegetables, and sauces on the table. Each person picks up a bite of food with chopsticks or a fondue fork, cooks it briefly in hot broth, then dips each bite in a sauce before eating. Toward the end of the meal, you add cooked noodles to the broth to make a soup.

Hot Pot Equipment

The most authentic container to hold the broth is a charcoal-fired Oriental hot pot available in Oriental hardware and import stores. A small one is used as a serving container for ginger beef in the photograph on page 23. Be sure to use one made of metal suitable for cooking, such as brass or stainless steel. Some are designed purely for ornamental use.

To fire a hot pot, fill the moat with hot cooking broth, then half fill the chimney with glowing charcoal. (Start charcoal briquets outdoors in a heavy bucket; transfer coals with tongs.) Be sure to put broth in the moat before adding coals, otherwise the heat of the charcoal may melt the pot's solder. *Warning:* Once filled with charcoal, the bottom of the hot pot becomes extremely hot, so protect your table surface well.

But you don't need a hot pot to stage this dinner. An electric frying pan is probably the easiest cooker to use because the heat is easily regulated. Or you could improvise a cooker using an alcohol burner and a 2-quart flameproof casserole.

Plan on four to six persons to share a cooking pot. For each place setting, provide a small plate for eating, individual dishes for sauces, a bowl for soup, and implements to pick up the food.

Selecting Ingredients

Most boneless tender meats, fish, poultry, and vegetables are suitable to cook in broth as long as they are cut in small pieces. Choose three or four meats and two or three vegetables from the following list: flank steak and boneless lean lamb, cut across the grain in ⅛-inch slices; chicken breast, skinned, boned, and cut in strips; small, raw shrimp, shelled and deveined; scallops, cut in half; oysters; bean curd or tofu, cut in 1-inch cubes; Chinese cabbage (napa cabbage) leaves, cut in 2-inch squares; spinach leaves, stems removed; sliced mushrooms; snow peas, ends and strings removed; asparagus, cut in 1-inch lengths; broccoli or cauliflower, cut in bite-size pieces; slivered green onions for garnish.

To estimate how many people your menu will serve, add up the total number of pounds of meat, poultry, seafood, and vegetables you plan to cook. Then allow a total of ¼ to ⅓ pound of meat, poultry, and seafood per person and a total of ⅓ pound vegetables per person.

Arrange each kind of food attractively on its own plate. If table space permits, you might set up two plates of each food so a complete selection is on either side of the cooking pot. Or arrange a combination plate of ingredients for each person. You can do this up to 8 hours ahead, then cover and chill.

You can make the chicken broth on page 24 or use canned broth. You will need enough to fill your cooking containers three-fourths full plus some extra to add as the foods cook.

Canned Chinese sauces are good to use as dipping sauces. Select two or three of the following: soy sauce, oyster sauce, plum sauce, hoisin sauce, and Chinese hot mustard (page 37), or chili oil (page 37).

For the end of the meal soup, cook Chinese noodles (page 81) or vermicelli; toss with a little sesame oil to prevent sticking. Allow ¼ pound uncooked noodles for each 4 persons. Cover and chill if cooked ahead, but bring to room temperature before adding to the broth.

Just before the meal starts, place the food and sauces on the table. Place the cooking container on the table and fill three-quarters full with boiling chicken broth; then seat the guests. Have more broth ready as needed. When dinner begins, each person picks up a bite of food and cooks it in the hot broth; most foods take 1 minute or less. The cooked foods are then dipped in one of the sauces and eaten. When guests have finished the meat and vegetables, add noodles to the broth, bring to boiling, then ladle into soup bowls.

2 cups broadleaf mustard (also called mustard cabbage), cut in 1-inch-thick slices, or 2 cups Chinese cabbage (napa cabbage), or regular cabbage, cut in 1-inch squares

1 can (about 8 oz.) abalone

About 4 cups chicken broth, page 24 or canned

1 teaspoon *each* dry sherry and soy sauce

¼ pound cooked ham, cut in thin slices

Salt and white pepper

Place mustard in a pan of boiling water for 1 minute to blanch; drain and rinse with cold water. (Do not blanch cabbage, if you use it.)

Drain and measure liquid from abalone. Combine liquid with enough chicken broth to make 5 cups and place in a 2-quart pan. Thinly slice abalone and reserve. Bring broth just to boiling. Add sherry, soy, and blanched mustard or raw cabbage. Simmer, uncovered, for 3 minutes. Add abalone and ham and simmer just long enough to heat through. Season with salt and pepper to taste. Makes 6 servings.

注意 **Chicken and mustard green soup.** Follow directions for abalone soup, but omit abalone. Increase **chicken broth** to 5 cups. Skin, bone and cut in bite-size pieces the meat from ½ pound **chicken breasts.** Blend 1 teaspoon *each* **cornstarch** and **dry sherry;** add chicken and stir to coat. Cook chicken in broth for 5 minutes before adding **mustard.**

Winter Melon Soup

If you live near an Oriental market, you can buy a whole winter melon to make this very special soup. And if you enjoy gardening, you can buy winter melon seeds to plant in late spring for a late fall harvest. Uncut winter melon can be stored in a warm dry place for several weeks without spoiling.

The Chinese like to serve winter melon soup as the first part of a multicourse dinner. Our version is thick and full—good enough to make a meal with an assort-

ment of cold appetizers.

Serving the soup in its large melon container is spectacular and showy. Chinese chefs often go one step further and carve a design, such as a writhing dragon or the symbol for good luck, on the outside of the melon. Any design can be carved with wood carving tools on the uncut melon one day ahead. The next day, cut off the top of the melon just before cooking.

Because the soup steams inside the whole melon, you'll need a large kettle with a rack in the bottom. A canning kettle works fine. It's a good idea to check the dimensions of your kettle and compare it to the size of the melon you plan to use. If the top of the melon extends slightly above the top of your kettle, you can improvise a lid from an overturned basket or a cap of foil, then cover the lid with towels to hold in the steam. In addition, you need a heatproof bowl that fits the melon base to hold it upright during the cooking and serving. You can make a sling with clean dishtowels to lower and raise the melon in the kettle.

3-pound broiler-fryer chicken, cut in pieces

1 fresh pork hock

2½ quarts water

1 pound chicken breasts

6 medium-size dried mushrooms

1 piece, about 1½ inches in diameter, dried tangerine peel, (optional)

2 ounces cooked ham

1 well shaped (about 10 lbs.) winter melon

2 quarter-size slices fresh ginger, crushed with the side of a cleaver

½ cup water chestnuts, sliced

½ cup sliced bamboo shoots

½ cup canned lotus seeds

1 tablespoon dry sherry

1 teaspoon sugar

Salt and white pepper

Reserve chicken breast from the cut up chicken. Place the remaining pieces in a large pan with the pork hock and water. Bring to a boil, skim off any foam, then reduce heat and simmer, covered,

for 2 hours. Add all the chicken breasts and continue simmering for 25 minutes.

Pour broth through a colander and reserve the pieces of chicken breast. Discard the remaining residue. When chicken breasts are cool enough to handle, remove meat from the bone, then skin, and cut in bite-size pieces. At this point you can refrigerate chicken meat and broth up to two days.

Cover mushrooms with warm water and let stand for 30 minutes. In a separate bowl, cover tangerine peel with warm water and let stand for 30 minutes. Drain mushrooms, cut off and discard stems, squeeze mushrooms dry, and thinly slice. Drain tangerine peel and scrape off inside of peel. Trim fat off ham and dice the lean meat. Cut top off melon and reserve; scoop out seeds and stringy portions. Place mushrooms inside of melon along with whole tangerine peel, ham, ginger, water chestnuts, bamboo shoots, and lotus seeds.

Skim fat off chicken broth. Reheat broth and season with sherry, sugar, and salt and pepper to taste. Set melon in a bowl, then set bowl in middle of a dishtowel and lower into the cooking pan with the rack in the bottom. Pour broth inside melon to fill it three-fourths full. Put top on melon, add enough water to pan to reach bottom of steaming rack. Cover pan and steam over low heat until melon meat is tender (about 3 to 4 hours). Replenish water in bottom of pan as it evaporates. Just before removing soup from heat, add the pieces of cooked chicken breast.

Lift melon out of pan; remove and discard tangerine peel and ginger. Spoon some of the soft flesh inside the melon into each bowl when you serve. Makes 6 main-course servings.

Save Peking duck bones to make elegant Duck Soup (page 25). Make-ahead Green Onion Cakes provide a delicious accompaniment (page 88).

Pork, Beef & Lamb

Are you accustomed to thinking of meat in the form of roasts, steaks, and chops? Most of us are. The Chinese, on the other hand, think of meat in terms of shreds, slices, and cubes. For Chinese cooks, it's a trade off—the more time spent in preparation means the less time spent in actual cooking.

The results, of course, are superb. Little nuggets of meat, stir-fried or deep-fried to succulence, are teamed up with vegetables or served alone, then coated with a flavorful sauce or light glaze. But just because the meat comes in small pieces doesn't mean the dish isn't filling. The recipes in this chapter are traditionally served as just one of the choices in a Chinese meal, but you'll find most of them satisfying and filling enough to stand as the main course in any meal.

Meat: Selecting & Slicing

When a recipe calls for boneless lean meat, you have several choices. With pork, the Chinese generally prefer to use well-trimmed pork butt or shoulder. While other cuts of pork may be leaner, they are not as tender and succulent when stir-fried. The favored cut for beef is flank steak. Its flat compact shape and texture make it easy to slice and juicy to cook. Top round, chuck roast, and beef sirloin can also be used.

Since many Chinese recipes call for small quantities of meat, it's best to plan for this by cutting the meat in small portions after you purchase it and then freezing the small portions separately. A flank steak, for example, can be cut in half lengthwise for two dishes, and a boneless pork butt can be cut to make 4 or 5 dishes. And if you slice the meat while it is still slightly frozen, you'll find the slicing is much easier.

When a recipe calls for chopped pork, the ground pork from most markets will work, but it usually contains a rather high percentage of fat. If you have a food processor, you can process pork butt yourself to make your own chopped pork. Cut the meat in 1-inch squares and process 1 cup at a time. (As with slicing, the meat chops more evenly if it is slightly frozen.)

Sweet & Sour Pork
Canton

There are endless variations of sweet and sour pork. This recipe combines crisply fried nuggets of pork with green pepper, onion, and pineapple in a sweet-sour sauce. Instead of the pineapple, you could also use canned lychees or mixed sweet pickles.

If you cook this for company, you may find it easier to deep-fry the pork ahead of time, then re-heat it before you add the sweet-sour cooking sauce.

Cooking sauce (directions follow)
1 egg yolk
2 teaspoons water
1 tablespoon *each* all-purpose flour and cornstarch
1 pound boneless lean pork, cut into 1-inch cubes
Salad oil
1 clove garlic, minced
1 green pepper, seeded and cut into 1-inch squares
1 medium-size onion, cut in wedges with layers separated
1 can (13 oz.) pineapple tidbits, drained

Prepare cooking sauce and set aside. In a bowl, beat egg yolk with water; blend in flour and cornstarch until smooth. Add cubes of pork and stir to coat.

In a deep pan, pour oil to a depth of about 1½ inches and heat to 340° on a deep-frying thermometer. Add meat and fry, stirring occasionally, until golden brown (about 10 to 12 minutes). Remove with a slotted spoon, drain, and keep warm. If made ahead, cool, cover, and refrigerate.

Heat a wok or wide frying pan over high heat. When pan is hot add 2 tablespoons oil. When oil begins to heat, add garlic and stir once. Add green pepper and onion and stir-fry for 1 minute, adding a few drops water if pan appears dry. Add pineapple and meat. Stir cooking sauce, add to pan, and cook, stirring, until sauce bubbles and thickens. Makes 4 servings.

Cooking sauce. In a bowl, combine ¾ cup **water** with 1 tablespoon *each* **cornstarch, catsup,** and **soy sauce;** 4 tablespoons *each* **sugar** and **wine vinegar;** and a few drops **liquid hot pepper seasoning.**

Twice Cooked Pork

Szechwan

Here is a very easy and delicious introduction to Szechwan cooking. Pork is simmered first in one piece, a day or two in advance, then it is sliced and stir-fried with green peppers and hot seasonings. You end up with a bonus of pork broth for soup, too.

1 pound boneless lean pork, in 1 piece
1 tablespoon dry sherry
1 quarter-size slice fresh ginger, crushed with the side of a cleaver
3 whole green onions
2 teaspoons hot bean sauce or 2 small, dry, hot chile peppers, crumbled and seeded (if desired)
4 teaspoons sweet bean sauce or hoisin sauce
1 tablespoon soy sauce
1 teaspoon sugar
2 small green peppers or 1 green and 1 red bell pepper
3 tablespoons salad oil
½ teaspoon salt
2 cloves garlic, minced
1 teaspoon minced fresh ginger

In a 2-quart pan, place pork, sherry, and the slice of ginger. Cut 1 of the green onions in half and add to pork. Add enough water to barely cover; bring meat to simmering. Cover and simmer until meat is tender when pierced with a fork (about 45 minutes). Remove meat from broth and chill.

When meat is cold, cut in 1½ by 1½-inch pieces ⅛-inch thick. The fatty parts of the meat are considered a delicacy, but remove them if you wish. In a bowl, combine the hot bean sauce or chile peppers, sweet bean sauce, soy, and sugar. Seed green peppers and cut in 1-inch squares. Cut the remaining 2 green onions in 1-inch lengths.

Heat a wok or wide frying pan over high heat. When pan is hot, add 2 tablespoons of the oil. When oil is hot, add peppers and stir-fry for 1½ minutes, adding a few drops water if pan appears dry. Sprinkle with salt, stir once, then remove peppers from pan. Add the remaining 1 tablespoon oil to pan. When oil begins to heat, add garlic and minced ginger. Stir once, then add pork and stir-fry for 1 minute. Add bean sauce mixture and toss until pork is coated with sauce. Return peppers to pan along with onion. Stir and cook for 30 seconds to heat through. Makes 3 or 4 servings.

Pearl Balls

As you might guess from the name, these are plump little meat balls with a special coating of glutinous rice. During steaming, the rice becomes translucent and pearl-like. Long-grain rice won't work as a substitute.

This recipe makes two batches of meatballs. If you don't have a tiered bamboo steamer which allows you to cook two layers at the same time, you can easily improvise steaming equipment. Support round cake racks 1 inch above boiling water in frying pans by resting the racks on clean, empty tuna cans with both ends opened.

⅔ cup glutinous rice
4 medium-size dried mushrooms
1 pound boneless lean pork, finely chopped or ground
¼ cup water chestnuts, finely chopped
1 whole green onion, finely chopped
1 egg
1 teaspoon *each* salt, cornstarch, and dry sherry
½ teaspoon grated fresh ginger
½ teaspoon crushed Szechwan peppercorns or ¼ teaspoon white pepper
½ teaspoon sugar
1 tablespoon soy sauce

Cover rice with cold water, let stand for 2 hours, then drain and spread on a plate. Cover mushrooms with warm water, let stand for 30 minutes, then drain. Cut off and discard stems; squeeze mushrooms dry and finely chop.

In a bowl, add mushrooms to pork along with water chestnuts and onion. Beat egg with salt, cornstarch, sherry, ginger, pepper, sugar, and soy. Add to meat and mix lightly.

With wet hands, roll meat mixture, 2 tablespoons at a time, into walnut-size balls. Roll each ball in glutinous rice to coat completely. Arrange balls (be sure they don't touch each other) on 2 heatproof plates that will fit inside your steamer. If done ahead, cover and refrigerate for as long as 8 hours.

(Continued on page 35)

Place plates on racks over boiling water. Drape a piece of wax paper over each plate. Cover steamer and cook, adding water as necessary to bottom of steamer, for 45 minutes or until meat is no longer pink. Makes 4 servings.

Mu Shu Pork

Peking (Pictured on page 39)

In the wheat growing areas of northern China, it is common to wrap a savory meat mixture in a paper thin pancake and eat it like a sandwich. Any filling coated with a minimum of sauce is suitable and mu shu pork, a combination of tender pork shreds, crisp vegetables, and creamy eggs, is one of the favorites. To add even more flavor, pungent hoisin sauce and shredded green onion are passed at the table so each person can season his sandwich to taste.

⅓ cup dried lily buds (also called golden needles)
4 dried black fungus or 4 medium-size dried mushrooms
1 teaspoon cornstarch
1 tablespoon *each* soy sauce and dry sherry
½ pound boneless lean pork, cut in matchstick pieces
3½ tablespoons salad oil
Cooking sauce (directions follow)
5 whole green onions
4 eggs, lightly beaten with ¼ teaspoon salt
½ teaspoon minced fresh ginger
½ cup sliced bamboo shoots, cut in matchstick pieces
1 small carrot, shredded
2 cups shredded iceberg lettuce
Hoisin sauce
Green onion brushes (directions follow)
About 18 mandarin pancakes (page 84)

Cover lily buds with warm water, let stand for 30 minutes, then drain. Cut off and discard hard tips

---

Garnished with tangy kumquat sauce, canned plum sauce, and catsup, Sweet & Sour Ribs (recipe on page 38) marinate overnight, then bake to succulence in the oven.

of buds, then cut each in half. Cover black fungus or dried mushrooms with warm water, let stand for 30 minutes, then drain. Cut off and discard hard knobby parts of fungus or cut off and discard mushroom stems; thinly slice.

In a bowl, combine cornstarch, soy, and sherry. Add pork and stir to coat. Stir in 1½ teaspoons of the oil. Let stand for 15 minutes to marinate.

Prepare cooking sauce and set aside. Cut onions in 1½-inch lengths; then cut lengthwise in thin shreds. Reserve half the green onion to pass at table; use other half for cooking.

Heat a wok or wide frying pan over medium-high heat. When pan is hot, add 1 tablespoon of the oil. When oil is hot, add eggs and cook, stirring, until softly set; then turn eggs out of pan.

Heat the remaining 2 tablespoons oil in pan and increase heat to high. When oil begins to heat, add ginger and stir once. Add pork and stir-fry until meat is lightly browned (about 4 minutes). Add lily buds and black fungus or mushrooms and stir-fry for 1 minute, adding 1 tablespoon water if pan appears dry. Add bamboo shoots, carrot, lettuce, ½ of the green onion, and cooking sauce and cook, stirring, until lettuce is crisp-tender (about 2 minutes). Add scrambled eggs to pan and break into bite-size pieces as you stir them into the meat mixture. When eggs are hot, turn into serving dish and serve at once.

Have on the table containers of hoisin sauce, the remaining shredded green onion, and green onion brushes. To eat, paint a little hoisin sauce on a mandarin pancake with a green onion brush, spoon on some meat mixture, garnish with shredded green onion, then wrap to enclose filling. Makes 4 to 6 servings.

Cooking sauce. In a bowl, combine 1 tablespoon *each* **soy sauce, dry sherry,** and **water;** 1 teaspoon *each* **sugar, cornstarch,** and **sesame oil;** and ¼ teaspoon **salt.**

Green onion brushes. Cut the white part of **green onions** in 1½-inch lengths. Using scissors or a sharp knife, slash each end of onion 3 or 4 times, cutting lengthwise into onion ½ inch. Cover onions with **ice water** and chill for 1 hour so edges curl.

注意 **Mu shu beef.** Follow directions for mu shu pork, but substitute ½ pound boneless lean **beef** for the pork. Stir-fry beef until browned on the outside but still pink within (about 1½ minutes). Remove beef from pan before stir-frying vegetables, then return to pan when you stir in the scrambled eggs.

Yu-shiang Pork

Szechwan (Pictured on page 86)

In Szechwan restaurants, this dish is also called pork with hot sauce or fish flavored pork. Yu-shiang style contains no fish, but calls for seasonings used in fish cookery, namely garlic and ginger. Expect a hot spicy flavor with undertones of sweet and sour. You can enjoy this pork three ways: stuff it in a crisp Chinese sesame bun, page 84; wrap it in a mandarin pancake, page 84; or eat with rice.

1 teaspoon cornstarch
¼ teaspoon salt
Dash of white pepper
1 tablespoon dry sherry
¾ pound boneless lean pork, cut in matchstick pieces
3½ tablespoons salad oil
Cooking sauce (directions follow)
2 cloves garlic, minced
1 teaspoon minced fresh ginger
3 or 4 small, dry, hot chile peppers
⅔ cup sliced bamboo shoots, cut in matchstick pieces
10 whole green onions, cut in 2-inch lengths

In a bowl, combine cornstarch, salt, pepper, and sherry. Add pork and stir to coat. Stir in 1½ teaspoons of the oil. Let stand for 15 minutes to marinate.

Prepare cooking sauce and set aside.

(Continued on next page)

Heat a wok or wide frying pan over high heat. When pan is hot, add 2 tablespoons of the oil. When oil begins to heat, add garlic, ginger, and chile peppers; stir once. Add pork and stir-fry until meat is lightly browned (about 4 minutes); remove from pan.

Heat the remaining 1 tablespoon oil in pan. Add bamboo shoots and onion and stir-fry for 1 minute. Return meat to pan. Stir cooking sauce, add to pan, and cook, stirring, until sauce bubbles and thickens. Makes 4 servings.

Cooking sauce. In a bowl, combine 1 tablespoon *each* **sugar, vinegar,** and **dry sherry;** 2 tablespoons **soy sauce;** 3 tablespoons **chicken broth** or water; and 2 teaspoons **cornstarch.**

注意 **Yu-shiang lamb.** Follow directions for yu-shiang pork, but substitute about 1¼ pounds **lamb shoulder** or loin chops for the pork. Cut meat off bones, trim off excess fat, and cut into matchstick pieces.

Cashew Pork

Match wedges with wedges, shreds with shreds, and cubes with cubes—this Chinese rule tells you how to slice and cut ingredients for a particular dish. In this case, cashews are a major ingredient, so the pork and vegetables are diced. The combination is rich and full of sweet nutty flavor.

- 2 teaspoons *each* cornstarch and soy sauce
- 1 tablespoon dry sherry
- ¾ pound boneless lean pork, cut in ½-inch cubes
- 3½ tablespoons salad oil
- 1 medium-size carrot, cut in ¼-inch cubes
  Cooking sauce (directions follow)
- 1 cup roasted cashews
- ½ teaspoon minced fresh ginger
- ½ cup diced bamboo shoots
- ⅓ cup frozen peas, thawed

In a bowl, combine cornstarch, soy, and sherry. Add pork and stir

to coat. Stir in 1½ teaspoons of the oil. Let stand for 15 minutes to marinate. Parboil carrot in water to cover for 5 minutes; drain. Prepare cooking sauce and set aside.

Heat a wok or wide frying pan over low heat. When pan is hot, add 1 tablespoon of the oil. When oil is hot, add cashews and stir-fry until golden (about 1 minute). Remove from pan and set aside. Increase heat to high and add the remaining 2 tablespoons oil. When oil begins to heat, add ginger and stir once. Add pork and stir-fry until meat is lightly browned (about 4 minutes). Add carrot, bamboo shoots, and peas and stir-fry for 1 minute. Stir cooking sauce, add to pan, and cook, stirring, until sauce bubbles and thickens. Makes 4 servings.

Cooking sauce. In a bowl, combine ⅓ cup **chicken broth** or water; 1 tablespoon *each* **vinegar, sugar, soy sauce,** and **hoisin sauce;** and ¼ teaspoon *each* **salt** and **sesame oil.**

Braised Pork with Chestnuts
Shanghai

Every cuisine has its exceptions and it is no different with the Chinese. They roast and braise larger pieces of meat, often using a technique called "red cooking." It is not a demanding technique. You simply simmer meat in a soy sauce mixture until tender and flavorful, then serve it when you wish—hot, cold, or reheated. This method is typical of Chinese home-style cooking, but restaurants that must turn out single orders with speed seldom take the time.

With red-cooked dishes you usually have a lot of sauce left over. Some cooks save the sauce and use it repeatedly; they call it master sauce. In this recipe, for example, you can strain the leftover sauce, then refrigerate or freeze it to use again.

The chestnuts in this dish lend a rich sweetness to the pork. Use fresh chestnuts when they are in season or dried chestnuts sold in Chinese markets. The dried ones give you year-round availability.

- 1 cup dried chestnuts or ½ pound fresh chestnuts
- 3 to 4 pounds boneless pork shoulder or butt, in 1 piece
- 3 cups water
- ⅓ cup *each* soy sauce and dry sherry
- 4 quarter-size slices fresh ginger, crushed with the side of a cleaver
- 1 large clove garlic, minced
- 4 whole green onions, cut in 2-inch lengths
- 2 tablespoons sugar

Cover dried chestnuts with hot water, let stand for 1 hour, then drain. Remove any skin from the creases. Cover again with water, simmer for 1 hour, then drain. If using fresh chestnuts, cut a slit on the flat side, then boil in water to cover for 10 minutes. Drain and, while still warm, peel; then remove inner skin.

In a 4-quart pan, place the pork, water, soy, sherry, ginger, garlic, onion, and sugar. Bring to a boil, then cover and simmer, turning meat occasionally, until very tender (about 2½ hours). Add dried chestnuts for the last 1 hour of cooking or add fresh chestnuts for the last 30 minutes of cooking. If made ahead, cool, cover, and refrigerate. Reheat by simmering in the sauce.

Lift meat from sauce and place on a serving dish. Remove chestnuts with a slotted spoon and place alongside pork. Skim off and discard fat from sauce, then strain sauce and pass to spoon over pork. Makes 10 to 12 servings.

Pork & Yams with Rice Crumbs
Szechwan

Toasted cream of rice cereal, used here in place of the traditional but hard-to-find rice powder, gives a

Mild or wild

We all have our own level of tolerance for hot, spicy food. What is tame and mild to one brings teary eyes and burning mouth to another. Throughout this book, we've adjusted the seasonings so the temperatures in spicy dishes are only mildly hot. If you wish to increase the heat, add one or more of the following condiments, which you can make at home and serve at the table for individual seasoning.

Hot Pepper & Black Bean Sauce

Hunan

Hot—hot and peppery—a little of this goes a long way with stir-fried dishes.

- 5 tablespoons salad oil
- 3 tablespoons crushed red pepper
- 1½ tablespoons fermented black beans, rinsed and drained
- 1½ tablespoons minced garlic
- 2 teaspoons *each* dry sherry and sesame oil
- ½ teaspoon salt

In a jar or bowl, place oil, red pepper, black beans, garlic, sherry, sesame oil, and salt. Cover tightly with foil. Set jar on rack over simmering water; cover and steam for 45 minutes. Cool, cover, and refrigerate indefinitely. Serve at room temperature. Makes ½ cup.

Hot Mustard

You can buy this in a jar, but it is easy to make in small quantities to enjoy at full potency. Served as a dip in small dishes, it is particularly good with deep-fried foods—egg roll, won ton, and batter-coated shrimp and chicken—and is often paired with catsup.

- ¼ cup dry mustard
- ⅓ cup cold water
- ⅛ teaspoon salad oil

Place mustard in a bowl. Gradually stir in cold water until smooth. Stir in oil. Cover and let stand for 1 hour for the flavor to mellow. Use immediately, or transfer to a small jar, cover, and refrigerate up to a month. Makes ⅓ cup.

Salt-Pepper Mix

Not as hot as black peppercorns, reddish-brown Szechwan peppercorns are wonderfully fragrant. When they are ground and mixed with salt, you have a zesty dip for deep-fried or roasted food, or you can use it as a table condiment.

- ¼ cup salt
- 1 tablespoon Szechwan peppercorns

In a wide frying pan over medium-low heat, heat salt and peppercorns, shaking pan occasionally, until the salt begins to brown and peppercorns become fragrant (about 10 minutes). Cool. Coarsely grind with a mortar and pestle or crush with a rolling pin. (Do not whirl in a blender.) Store in a covered jar at room temperature. Makes ¼ cup.

Chili Oil

For sparkling hot flavor, add a few drops of this oil while cooking stir-fried dishes, or pass at the table in a small cruet. It is good with noodles or steamed dim sum, especially when used with vinegar and soy sauce.

- ½ cup salad oil *or* ⅓ cup salad oil and 3 tablespoons sesame oil
- 6 small, dry, hot chile peppers *or* 2 tablespoons crushed red pepper

In a small pan, heat oil over medium heat. When oil is hot but not smoking, add chile peppers and stir for 1 minute. Remove from heat and cool. Strain and discard peppers. Store in a covered jar at room temperature. Makes ½ cup.

Hot Pepper Oil

For extra zing, add a few drops of this oil to any stir-fried dish.

- 2 tablespoons Szechwan peppercorns
- ½ cup salad oil
- ½ teaspoon *each* paprika and ground red pepper (cayenne)

In a wide frying pan over medium-low heat, heat peppercorns, shaking pan occasionally, until fragrant (about 10 minutes). Cool. Coarsely grind with a mortar and pestle or crush with a rolling pin. Heat salad oil until hot; pour over peppercorns, then stir in paprika and red pepper. Cool. Strain oil, discarding peppercorns. Store in a covered jar at room temperature. Makes ½ cup.

fluffy coating to this combination of pork and yams. The sauce is more deeply savory than searingly hot. You could serve this without the yams (or the variation with beef that follows) as a hot appetizer. For a complete meal, serve the pork and yams with rice and stir-fried spinach.

    3   tablespoons cream of rice cereal
    1½ tablespoons *each* soy sauce, dry
        sherry, and salad oil
    1   tablespoon sweet bean sauce
    1   teaspoon *each* minced fresh ginger
        and garlic
    1   teaspoon hot bean sauce *or* ¼
        teaspoon liquid hot pepper
        seasoning
    ¼   teaspoon sesame oil
        Dash of white pepper
    1   pound boneless lean pork, cut in
        ½-inch cubes
    2   medium-size (about 1 lb.) yams
    1   tablespoon dry sherry
    ¼   teaspoon salt
    2   whole green onions, thinly sliced

In a small frying pan, toast cream of rice over medium heat, shaking pan occasionally, until cereal is lightly browned (about 5 minutes). Cool.

In a bowl, combine soy, the 1½ tablespoons sherry, salad oil, sweet bean sauce, ginger, garlic, hot bean sauce, sesame oil, pepper, and 2 tablespoons of the toasted cream of rice. Add pork and stir to coat. Cover and marinate in the refrigerator for 4 hours or until next day.

Peel yams and cut in ½-inch-thick slices. Blend the remaining 1 tablespoon cream of rice with the 1 tablespoon sherry and ¼ teaspoon salt; mix with yams to coat.

Arrange pork cubes in heatproof 1-quart casserole; distribute yam mixture on top. Place casserole on rack in a steamer over boiling water. Drape a piece of wax paper over casserole, cover steamer, and cook, adding water as necessary to bottom of steamer, for 40 minutes or until pork and yams are fork-tender. Remove casserole from steamer and let stand for a few minutes, then invert onto a serving plate. Scatter green onions over the top. Makes 4 or 5 servings.

注意 **Beef with rice crumbs.** Follow directions for pork with rice crumbs, but substitute 1 pound **flank steak,** cut in 1-inch squares, for the pork and eliminate the yams with their coating of sherry, salt, and cream of rice. Steam meat for 40 minutes or until beef is fork-tender, then invert on a **lettuce**-lined plate before sprinkling with green onion.

Black Bean Spareribs with Green Peppers
Canton

Redolent with black beans and garlic, this dish is definitely not for a formal meal. For a casual occasion you might serve this with cold spiced shrimp (page 60), sprout and cress salad (page 77), and plenty of rice. The Chinese have a knack for holding spareribs with chopsticks and eating the meat off the bone, but you may find it easier to use your fingers. Provide plenty of napkins and set a small bowl on the table for bones.

    ½   side (about 1½ lbs.) pork
        spareribs, cut in 1-inch lengths
    4   tablespoons salad oil
    3   tablespoons water
    2   tablespoons fermented black
        beans, rinsed, drained, and
        finely chopped
    2   large cloves garlic, minced
    1   small, dry, hot chile pepper,
        crumbled and seeded, if desired
    2   green peppers, seeded and cut in
        1-inch squares
    ¼   cup water
    1   tablespoon soy sauce

Trim excess fat from ribs, then cut between the bones to make individual pieces. Heat a wok or wide frying pan over high heat. When pan is hot, add 2 tablespoons of the oil. When oil is hot, add ribs and stir-fry until lightly browned (about 4 minutes). Add the 3 tablespoons water, reduce heat to low, cover, and cook, stirring occasionally, until tender when pierced (about 30 minutes). Remove ribs from pan and discard pan drippings.

Add the remaining 2 tablespoons oil to pan and increase heat to high. When oil begins to heat, add black beans, garlic, and chile pepper. Stir-fry for 5 seconds, then add green peppers and stir-fry for 30 seconds. Add ribs, the ¼ cup water, and soy. Cover and cook for 2 minutes. Remove cover and continue cooking until all liquid evaporates. Makes 3 or 4 servings.

Sweet & Sour Ribs with Kumquat Sauce
Canton   (Pictured on page 34)

An apricot-based marinade gives a fruity sweetness to these tender, succulent spareribs. There is more than enough marinade in the recipe, so if you don't use it all, you can keep it in the refrigerator for 2 weeks or freeze for longer storage, and use again with pork or the variations that follow. Pass kumquat sauce at the table.

    1   small can (8 oz.) apricot halves
    1½ tablespoons coarsely chopped
        fresh ginger
    2   whole cloves garlic, peeled
    1   teaspoon Chinese five-spice
    2   tablespoons white vinegar
    ¼   cup soy sauce
    3   tablespoons *each* bean sauce and
        sugar
    ½   cup *each* catsup and hoisin sauce
    2   large sides (about 4 lbs.) pork
        spareribs
        Sweet and sour kumquat sauce
        (directions follow)

In a blender, whirl the apricots (including syrup), ginger, garlic, five-spice, and vinegar until smooth. Add the soy, bean sauce, sugar, catsup, and hoisin sauce. Whirl until blended.

(Continued on page 40)

Make a Peking-style sandwich with a Mandarin Pancake wrapper (recipe on page 84) and a savory Mu Shu Pork filling (recipe on page 35). For an easy meal, serve with Egg Drop Soup (recipe on page 28).

Trim excess fat from spareribs. Place ribs in a large shallow baking pan; pour marinade over ribs and turn meat to coat all sides. Cover and refrigerate for 6 hours or overnight, turning occasionally.

Remove ribs from marinade, drain well, and place on racks over foil-lined baking pans. Bake in a 350° oven for 30 minutes. Turn meat over and continue baking until tender when pierced (about 40 minutes). Brush occasionally with marinade during the last 20 minutes of baking. Cut spareribs into serving-size pieces before serving. Pass kumquat sauce at the table to spoon over ribs. Makes 8 servings.

Sweet and sour kumquat sauce. In a pan, bring ¾ cup *each* **sugar** and **white wine vinegar** to a boil. When sugar dissolves, remove from heat and cool. Drain 1 jar (14 oz.) **kumquats;** cut kumquats in half lengthwise and remove seeds. In a blender, whirl sugar-vinegar mixture, 1 can (about 1 lb.) drained **apricot halves** (reserve and add ½ cup of the syrup if you want a more subtle flavor), and 1 small can (8 oz.) **applesauce** until smooth. Add 1 small jar (2 oz.) diced **pimentos** (drained) and kumquats. Blend until coarsely chopped. Sauce will keep for 1 month in the refrigerator. Makes about 3½ cups.

注意 **Sweet & sour steak.** Follow directions for spareribs, but substitute 1 large (about 2 pounds) **flank steak** for the spareribs. With a sharp knife, score the steak on one side by making cuts lengthwise and crosswise about ¼ inch deep at ½-inch intervals. Place steak on a rack over a foil-lined broiler pan. Rub about 1 cup marinade well into both sides of meat. Cover and refrigerate for 2 to 4 hours. Broil steak (still on rack in pan) about 4 inches from heat, turning once, for about 8 minutes for medium rare or until as done as you like. Brush meat occasionally with marinade as it broils. Cut into 3-inch squares and serve with

sweet and sour kumquat sauce. Makes 5 or 6 servings.

注意 **Sweet & sour baked chicken.** Follow directions for spareribs, but substitute for the spareribs 1 large (about 3½ lbs.) broiler-fryer **chicken** cut in serving-size pieces. Place chicken in a shallow dish; pour 2 cups of the marinade over chicken. Cover and refrigerate for 4 to 6 hours, turning several times. Drain chicken and arrange on a rack over a foil-lined broiler pan. Bake in a 400° oven for 55 to 60 minutes or until no longer pink when slashed near the bone. Turn once and brush occasionally with marinade during the last 30 minutes. Serve with sweet and sour kumquat sauce. Makes 4 or 5 servings.

Stir-fried Pork with Corn

Canton

Sold in cans or jars, whole baby sweet corn, also called midget sweet corn, is so tender that you eat the cob, too.

- 1 teaspoon *each* cornstarch and soy sauce
- 1 tablespoon dry sherry
- ¼ teaspoon pepper
- 1 pound boneless lean pork, cut in 1 by 2-inch strips ⅛ inch thick
- 4 tablespoons salad oil
 Cooking sauce (directions follow)
- 2 cloves garlic, minced
- 1 small onion, cut in wedges with layers separated
- ¼ pound fresh mushrooms, thinly sliced
- 1 can (about 1 lb.) whole baby sweet corn, drained
- 8 whole green onions, cut in 2-inch lengths

In a bowl, combine the cornstarch, soy, sherry, and pepper. Add pork and stir to coat. Stir in 1 teaspoon of the oil. Let stand for 15 minutes to marinate.

Prepare cooking sauce and set aside.

Heat a wok or wide frying pan over high heat. When pan is hot,

add about 2 tablespoons of the oil. When oil begins to heat, add garlic and stir once. Add ½ the pork mixture and stir-fry until meat is lightly browned (about 4 minutes); remove from pan. Repeat, using another tablespoon oil and remaining meat.

Heat the remaining oil in pan. Add onion wedges and mushrooms and stir-fry for 1 minute, adding a few drops water if pan appears dry. Add corn, pork, and green onion and cook for 30 seconds. Stir cooking sauce, add to pan, and cook, stirring, until sauce bubbles and thickens. Makes 4 servings.

Cooking sauce. In a bowl, combine 1½ tablespoons **cornstarch,** 1 teaspoon *each* **sugar** and **vinegar,** ¼ teaspoon **salt,** 1 tablespoon **soy sauce,** and ¾ cup **chicken broth** or **water.**

Green Pepper Beef

Canton   (Pictured on page 78)

Stir-frying beef with vegetables is one of the most delicious and versatile Chinese techniques to master. You marinate thin strips of beef to give them flavor and a smooth coating. Next you cook the strips quickly, combining them with a vegetable of your choice. The basic recipe given here will get you started.

 About ¾ pound boneless lean beef
- 1 tablespoon *each* dry sherry, soy sauce, and water
- ¼ teaspoon *each* salt and sugar
- 2 teaspoons cornstarch
- 3½ tablespoons salad oil
 Cooking sauce (directions follow)
- 1 clove garlic, minced
- ½ teaspoon minced fresh ginger
- 2 small green peppers, seeded and cut in ¼-inch-wide strips
- 1 tablespoon water
- ¼ teaspoon salt

Cut beef with the grain into 1½-inch-wide strips. Cut each strip across the grain in ⅛-inch-thick slanting slices. In a bowl, combine the sherry, soy, the 1 tablespoon water, ¼ teaspoon salt, sugar, and cornstarch. Add beef and stir to coat, then stir in 1½ teaspoons of the oil and let stand for 15 minutes to marinate.

Prepare cooking sauce and set aside.

Heat a wok or wide frying pan over high heat. When pan is hot, add 2 tablespoons of the oil. When oil begins to heat, add garlic and ginger and stir once. Add beef and stir-fry until meat is browned on the outside but still pink within (about 1½ minutes); remove from pan.

Heat the remaining 1 tablespoon oil. Add green pepper and stir-fry for 30 seconds. Add the other 1 tablespoon water and ¼ teaspoon salt, cover, and cook for 1 minute. Return meat to pan. Stir cooking sauce, add to pan, and cook, stirring, until sauce bubbles and thickens. Makes 4 servings.

Cooking sauce. In a bowl, combine 1 tablespoon *each* **soy sauce** and **cornstarch** and ½ cup **chicken broth** or water. (If you plan to serve this in the phoenix nest pictured in page 78, be sure to prepare only half the cooking sauce.)

注意 **Ginger beef.** (Pictured on page 23) Follow directions for green pepper beef, but substitute 2 whole **green onions** (cut in 1½-inch lengths) for the green peppers and 2 tablespoons slivered fresh **ginger** for the minced ginger. Stir-fry meat for 1½ minutes, add green onion, and continue cooking for 30 seconds before adding cooking sauce.

注意 **Oyster beef.** Follow directions for green pepper beef, but substitute ½ cup sliced **bamboo shoots** and 6 medium-size **dried mushrooms** for the green peppers. Cover mushrooms with warm **water,** let stand for 30 minutes, then drain. Cut off and discard stems; squeeze mushrooms dry and thinly slice. After removing beef from pan, stir-fry bamboo shoots and mushrooms for 1 min-

ute. Add 1 tablespoon **water,** cover, and cook for 2 minutes before returning beef to pan. Substitute 2 tablespoons **oyster sauce** for the 1 tablespoon soy in the cooking sauce.

注意 **Two-onion beef.** Follow directions for green pepper beef, but substitute 1 large **onion** and 12 whole **green onions** for the green pepper. Cut onion in half, then thinly slice; cut green onion in 1½-inch lengths. After removing beef from pan, stir-fry thinly sliced onion for 1 minute. Add green onion and stir-fry for 30 seconds before returning beef to pan.

Dry-fried Beef
Szechwan

Part of the intrigue of Chinese food comes from a surprise in texture as well as taste. In this recipe, shreds of beef are deep-fried so they are crisp and chewy rather than silky and tender, then they are tumbled with vegetables and seasonings that are sweet, salty, and spicy.

¾	**pound boneless lean beef**
1	**tablespoon hot bean sauce**
1	**tablespoon dry sherry**
½	**teaspoon sugar**
1	**or 2 small, dry, hot chile peppers,** crumbled and seeded (if desired)
½	**cup salad oil**
1	**large stalk celery, cut in matchstick pieces**
1	**medium-size carrot, cut in matchstick pieces**
2	**teaspoons minced garlic**
1	**teaspoon minced fresh ginger**
2	**whole green onions, cut in** 1½-inch lengths
1	**teaspoon sesame oil**
½	**teaspoon Szechwan peppercorns,** roasted and crushed (page 14)

Cut meat in slices ⅛ inch thick, then cut into shreds ⅛ inch wide and 2 inches long. In a bowl, combine the hot bean sauce, sherry, sugar, and chile peppers; set aside.

Pour salad oil in a wok or small deep pan and heat over medium-

high heat to 360° on a deep-frying thermometer. Add ½ the meat and stir to separate shreds. Cook until meat is dark brown, slightly shriveled, and chewy (about 2½ to 3 minutes). Remove with a slotted spoon and drain on paper towels. Reheat oil to 360° and repeat with remainder of the meat.

Pour off all but 3 tablespoons oil. (If you deep-fried in a pan, pour 3 tablespoons of the oil into a wide frying pan.) Increase heat to high. When oil is hot, add celery and carrot and stir-fry for 2 minutes. Add garlic and ginger and stir-fry for 30 seconds. Add onion and stir-fry for 30 seconds. Return meat to pan, add hot bean sauce mixture, and cook, stirring, until most of the liquid has evaporated. Stir in sesame oil and crushed peppercorns before serving. Makes 4 to 6 servings.

Tomato Beef
Canton   (Pictured on page 42)

These tender strips of beef are paired with a variety of colorful, crisp vegetables and tossed with a curry-flavored sauce. For an easy meal, all you need to add is steamed rice.

¾	**pound boneless lean beef**
2	**teaspoons** *each* **cornstarch and** soy sauce
1	**tablespoon** *each* **dry sherry and** water
¼	**teaspoon salt**
4	**tablespoons salad oil** Cooking sauce (directions follow)
½	**teaspoon minced fresh ginger**
1	**clove garlic, minced**
2	**large stalks celery, cut in** ¼-inch-thick slanting slices
1	**medium-size onion, cut in wedges** with layers separated
1	**green pepper, seeded and cut in** 1-inch squares
3	**medium-size tomatoes, each cut in** 6 wedges

Cut beef with the grain into 1½-inch-wide strips. Cut each strip across the grain in ⅛-inch-thick slanting slices. In a bowl, combine cornstarch, soy, sherry, water, and

salt. Add beef and stir to coat, then stir in 1½ teaspoons of the oil and let stand for 15 minutes to marinate.

Prepare cooking sauce and set aside.

Heat a wok or wide frying pan over high heat. When pan is hot, add 2 tablespoons of the oil. When oil begins to heat, add ginger and garlic and stir once. Add beef and stir-fry until meat is browned on the outside but still pink within (about 1½ minutes); remove from pan.

Heat the remaining 1½ tablespoons oil. Add celery and onion and stir-fry for 1 minute. Add green pepper and stir-fry for 1 minute, adding a few drops water if pan appears dry. Add tomatoes and stir-fry for 1 minute. Return meat to pan. Stir cooking sauce, add to pan, and cook, stirring, until sauce bubbles and thickens. Makes 4 servings.

Cooking sauce. In a bowl, combine 1 tablespoon *each* **soy sauce, Worcestershire,** and **cornstarch,** 3 tablespoons **catsup,** 1 teaspoon **curry powder,** and ½ cup **water.**

注意 **Tomato-beef chow mein.** Follow directions for tomato beef, then serve over **pan fried noodles** (page 81).

Liver with Mushrooms & Onions

Liver and onions are compatible partners in any cuisine. Chinese style, beef liver is cut in thin strips, then stir-fried so it is seared on the outside but juicy within. Smoky dried mushrooms give depth to the flavor.

A trademark of Cantonese cooks, Tomato Beef (recipe on page 41), flavored with curry and served with rice, is satisfying enough to make a whole meal.

6 medium-size dried mushrooms
⅔ pound sliced beef liver
3 tablespoons salad oil
½ teaspoon minced fresh ginger
1 large onion, cut in half lengthwise and thinly sliced
5 whole green onions, cut in 1½-inch lengths
2 tablespoons dry sherry
1 tablespoon soy sauce
½ teaspoon sugar
¼ teaspoon salt

Cover mushrooms with warm water and let stand for 30 minutes. Reserve 3 tablespoons of the soaking liquid and pour off the remainder. Cut off and discard stems; squeeze mushrooms dry and thinly slice. Remove membrane from liver, if necessary. Cut liver lengthwise in 1½-inch-wide strips, then cut crosswise in ⅛-inch-thick slices.

Heat a wok or wide frying pan over high heat. When pan is hot, add 2 tablespoons of the oil. When oil begins to heat, add ginger and stir once. Add liver and stir-fry until browned on the outside but still juicy within (about 1½ minutes); remove from pan.

Add the remaining 1 tablespoon oil to pan. Add mushrooms and stir-fry for 1 minute. Add the 3 tablespoons mushroom soaking liquid, cover, and cook for 3 minutes. Add thinly sliced onion and green onion and stir-fry for 1 minute. Add sherry, soy, sugar, and salt and stir-fry for 1 minute. Return liver to pan and continue stir-frying until most of the liquid has evaporated. Makes 3 servings.

Mongolian Grill

Mongolian grill is a pleasant way to entertain informally. You can prepare the ingredients and sauces a day ahead; later, your guests can choose and cook their own food.

This type of food originally was cooked on a slotted, dome-shaped charcoal grill. The easiest way to cook it when entertaining, is to use an electric griddle or an electric frying pan.

3 pounds lamb shoulder chops or 2 pounds boneless lean beef or a combination of both
3 large carrots, shredded
2 large onions, thinly sliced
¾ pound bean sprouts, washed and drained
2 green peppers, seeded and cut in ¼-inch-wide strips
3 cups shredded cabbage
Seasoning sauces (directions follow)
Salad oil
12 Chinese sesame buns (page 84)

Trim excess fat from meat; cut meat from the bone. Slice meat across the grain into strips ¼ inch thick and 2 to 3 inches long. Place meats, vegetables, and sauces in separate bowls.

At serving time, preheat electric griddle to 350°. For each serving, have guests select about 1 cup of mixed vegetables, douse them with 1 or 2 teaspoons of each seasoning sauce, then select several slices of meat. Brush griddle with about 1 teaspoon oil and put on meats. Cook meat, turning, until lightly browned (about 1 minute); add vegetables and seasonings. Continue cooking, stirring meat and vegetables until vegetables are just tender (about 1 minute). Stuff into Chinese sesame bun and eat out of hand or serve with rice. Makes about 2 servings for each of 6 persons.

Hot chile sauce. Mix 1 teaspoon **chili oil** (page 37 or bottled) or 1½ teaspoons liquid hot pepper seasoning with ¾ cup **soy sauce.**

Garlic sauce. Using a mortar and pestle, crush 1½ teaspoons minced **garlic** with 1 teaspoon **salt** to make a smooth paste. Stir in ⅓ cup **white wine vinegar** and 2 tablespoons **water** until well blended.

Lemon-ginger sauce. Grate 1 teaspoon peel from 2 large **lemons;** set aside. Cut off all the white membrane from lemons, then thinly slice and remove seeds. Thinly slice a 1-inch piece of peeled fresh **ginger** and place in a blender with lemon slices, the grated peel , and ¼ cup **water.** Purée until smooth.

Chicken & Duck

Chinese ways with poultry are so diverse that one's taste cannot help but be satisfied. Succulent morsels are stir-fried with vegetables, larger pieces are cloaked in crisp batter and crowned with a shimmering sauce, whole plump birds are braised and roasted.

If you are new to Chinese cooking, and particularly stir-frying, preparing poultry is a good way to start. Chicken cooks quickly and the technique is easy to master on the first try. But first a word about cutting poultry. Because Chinese food is meant to be eaten with chopsticks, chicken and duck that is not boned is usually hacked with a cleaver into bite-size pieces. Even professional chefs sometimes end up with small splinters of bone—an unpleasant surprise for the unsuspecting diner. You may prefer to cut poultry in the more traditional manner, but you'll still enjoy the same delicious flavors.

Chicken & Snow Peas

Canton (Pictured on page 47)

A meat, a marinade, and a cooking sauce—that's the basis for dozens of stir-fried dishes. What you pair with the meat is largely a matter of personal taste and seasonal availability. To get you started, we give directions here for chicken and snow peas, then tell you how you can change the recipe to make other Cantonese favorites. As with most Chinese recipes, the proportion of meat to vegetables is flexible.

- 4 medium-size dried mushrooms
- 2 teaspoons *each* soy sauce, cornstarch, dry sherry, and water
  Dash of white pepper
- 1½ pounds chicken breasts, skinned, boned, and cut in bite-size pieces
- 3½ tablespoons salad oil
  Cooking sauce (directions follow)
- 1 small clove garlic, minced
- ½ cup sliced bamboo shoots
- ¼ pound snow peas, ends and strings removed

Cover mushrooms with warm water, let stand for 30 minutes, then drain. Cut off and discard stems; squeeze mushrooms dry, thinly slice, and set aside. In a bowl, combine soy, cornstarch, sherry, water, and pepper. Add chicken and toss to coat, then stir in 1½ teaspoons of the oil and let stand for 15 minutes to marinate. Prepare cooking sauce and set aside.

Place a wok or wide frying pan over high heat. When pan is hot, add 2 tablespoons of the oil. When oil begins to heat, add garlic and stir once. Add chicken and stir-fry until chicken is opaque (about 3 minutes). Remove chicken from pan.

Add the remaining 1 tablespoon oil to pan. When oil is hot, add mushrooms and bamboo shoots. Stir-fry for 1 minute, adding a few drops water if pan appears dry. Add snow peas and stir-fry for 1½ minutes, adding a few drops more water if pan appears dry. Return chicken to pan. Stir cooking sauce, add to pan, and cook, stirring, until sauce bubbles and thickens. Makes 3 or 4 servings.

Cooking sauce. Mix together ½ cup **water**, 1 tablespoon **dry sherry**, 2 tablespoons **oyster sauce** or soy sauce, ¼ teaspoon **sugar**, 1 teaspoon **sesame oil**, and 1 tablespoon **cornstarch**.

注意 **Cashew or almond chicken.** Follow directions for chicken and snow peas, but first toast ½ cup **cashews** or blanched **almonds** in 1 tablespoon **salad oil** over medium-low heat until golden; remove from pan and set aside. In same pan, stir-fry chicken as directed. Stir in nuts just before serving.

注意 **Chicken & zucchini.** Follow directions for chicken and snow peas, but eliminate bamboo shoots and substitute 1 pound **zucchini** for the snow peas. Roll-cut zucchini (pictured page 72) by making a diagonal slice straight down through zucchini, then rolling zucchini ¼ turn and slicing again. Stir-fry zucchini with mushrooms for 30 seconds, add 2 tablespoons **water**, cover, and cook until crisp-tender (about 3 minutes); then return chicken to pan.

注意 **Chicken & peppers.** Follow directions for chicken and snow peas, but substitute 2 **green peppers**, seeded and cut in 1-inch squares, for the snow peas.

Asparagus Chicken with Black Bean Sauce

Canton   (Pictured on page 10)

Here is a perfect way to celebrate fresh asparagus, and to discover the flexibility of a Chinese recipe, not to mention the stir-fry technique. Following the same steps, you can use zucchini for the vegetable when asparagus is past its prime, then when green or red bell peppers are plentiful, you can treat them the same way. You can even adjust the ratio of chicken to vegetables, increasing or decreasing one or the other to suit your mood and taste.

 1 teaspoon *each* cornstarch and soy sauce
 2 teaspoons dry sherry
 1 teaspoon water
 1 pound chicken breasts, skinned, boned, and cut in bite-size pieces
 3½ tablespoons salad oil
    Cooking sauce (directions follow)
 1 pound asparagus
 2 teaspoons fermented black beans, rinsed, drained, and finely chopped
 1 large clove garlic, minced
 1 medium-size onion, cut in wedges with layers separated
 2 tablespoons water

In a bowl, combine cornstarch, soy, sherry, and the 1 teaspoon water. Add chicken and stir to coat, then stir in 1½ teaspoons of the oil and let stand for 15 minutes to marinate.

Prepare cooking sauce and set aside. Wash asparagus and break off tough ends; cut in ½-inch slanting slices.

Heat a wok or wide frying pan over high heat. When pan is hot, add 2 tablespoons of the oil. When oil begins to heat, add black beans and garlic; stir once. Add chicken and stir-fry until chicken is opaque (about 3 minutes). Remove chicken from pan.

Add the remaining 1 tablespoon oil to pan. When oil is hot, add asparagus and onion and stir-fry for 30 seconds. Add the 2 tablespoons water, cover, and cook, stirring occasionally, until crisp-tender (about 2 minutes). Return chicken to pan. Stir cooking sauce, add to pan, and cook, stirring, until sauce bubbles and thickens. Makes 3 or 4 servings.

Cooking sauce. In a small bowl, combine 1 tablespoon *each* **soy sauce** and **cornstarch**, ¼ teaspoon **sugar**, and ½ cup **chicken broth** or water.

注意 **Asparagus beef with black bean sauce.** Follow directions for asparagus chicken, but substitute ¾ pound boneless lean **beef**, such as flank or round steak, for the chicken. Cut meat with the grain in 1½-inch-wide strips, then cut each strip across the grain in ⅛-inch-thick slanting slices. Increase **water** in marinade to 1 tablespoon. Stir-fry meat until browned on the outside and pink in the middle (about 1½ minutes).

注意 **Asparagus shrimp with black bean sauce.** Follow directions for asparagus chicken, but substitute 1 pound medium-size raw **shrimp** (shelled and deveined) for the chicken. Stir-fry shrimp until they turn pink (about 3 minutes).

Kung Pao Chicken
Szechwan

This quick stir-fry is one of the most popular exports from the region of Szechwan. Charred dried chile peppers give breathtaking fire to tender morsels of chicken. In China, the peppers are eaten along with the chicken, but unless you like very hot food, you may prefer to set them aside.

Watch the chile peppers closely as they cook. If they burn, they release potent volatile oils which sting the nose and eyes.

 1   tablespoon *each* dry sherry and cornstarch
 ½   teaspoon salt
 ⅛   teaspoon white pepper
 1½ pounds chicken breasts, skinned, boned, and cut in bite-size pieces
 4   tablespoons salad oil
     Cooking sauce (directions follow)
 4   to 6 small, dry, hot chile peppers
 ½   cup salted peanuts
 1   teaspoon *each* minced garlic and fresh ginger
 2   whole green onions, cut in 1½-inch lengths

In a bowl, combine sherry, cornstarch, salt, and pepper. Add chicken and stir to coat, then stir in 1 tablespoon of the oil and let stand for 15 minutes to marinate. Prepare cooking sauce and set aside.

Heat a wok or wide frying pan over medium heat. When pan is

hot, add 1 tablespoon of the oil. Add whole peppers and peanuts and cook, stirring, until peppers just begin to char. If peppers become completely black, discard. Remove peanuts from pan and repeat with new peppers. Remove from pan and set aside.

Add remaining 2 tablespoons oil to pan and increase heat to high. When oil begins to heat, add garlic and ginger. Stir once, then add chicken and stir-fry until chicken is opaque (about 3 minutes). Add peppers, peanuts, and onion to pan. Stir cooking sauce, add to pan, and cook, stirring, until sauce bubbles and thickens. Makes 4 to 6 servings.

Cooking sauce. In a bowl, combine 2 tablespoons **soy sauce**, 1 table-spoon *each* **white wine vinegar** and **dry sherry**, 3 tablespoons **chicken broth** or water, and 2 teaspoons *each* **sugar** and **cornstarch**.

注意 **Kung pao shrimp.** (Pictured on cover) Follow directions for kung pao chicken, but substitute 1½ pounds medium-size raw **shrimp** (shelled and deveined) for the chicken. Stir-fry shrimp until they turn pink (about 2 minutes).

注意 **Kung pao scallops.** Follow directions for kung pao chicken, but substitute 1¼ pounds raw **scallops** (cut in ¼-inch-thick slices) for the chicken. Stir-fry until they turn opaque (about 2 minutes).

Hot & Sour Chicken

Hunan

Crushed red pepper makes this dish hot; vinegar provides the classic sour balance. By Hunanese standards, this dish is mildly seasoned. If you like food that produces watery eyes and burning mouth, pass a little bowl of hot pepper and black bean sauce, chili oil, or hot pepper oil (page 37) to make it as hot as you want.

2 teaspoons *each* cornstarch and dry sherry
¼ teaspoon *each* salt and pepper
1 pound chicken breasts, skinned, boned, and cut in bite-size pieces
About 3½ tablespoons salad oil
Cooking sauce (directions follow)
1 tablespoon minced garlic
2 teaspoons minced fresh ginger
1 tablespoon fermented black beans, rinsed and drained
1 small green pepper, seeded and cut in 1-inch squares
1 medium-size carrot, thinly sliced
1 can (about 8 oz.) sliced bamboo shoots
1 tablespoon water

In a bowl, combine cornstarch, sherry, salt, and pepper. Add chicken and stir to coat, then stir in 1½ teaspoons of the oil and let stand for 15 minutes to marinate. Prepare cooking sauce and set aside.

Place a wok or wide frying pan over high heat. When pan is hot, add 2 tablespoons of the oil. When oil begins to heat, add garlic, ginger, and black beans. Stir once, then add chicken and stir-fry until chicken is opaque (about 3 minutes). Remove chicken from pan.

Add the remaining 1 tablespoon oil to pan. When oil is hot, add green pepper, carrot, and bamboo shoots. Stir-fry for 30 seconds. Add water and stir-fry for 1½ minutes. Return chicken to pan. Stir cooking sauce, add to pan, and cook, stirring, until sauce bubbles and thickens. Makes 4 servings.

Cooking sauce. In a bowl, mix together 2 teaspoons **cornstarch**, ½ teaspoon *each* **crushed red pepper** and **salad oil**, 2 tablespoons **soy sauce**, 2½ tablespoons **white wine vinegar**, and ½ cup **chicken broth** or water.

Chicken with Peking Sauce

Peking   (Pictured on page 86)

Canned hoisin sauce gives the characteristic spicy sweet flavor and rich dark color to this dish

glazed in the Peking style. You can serve it with rice, but it is especially delicious as a filling for the Chinese sesame buns on page 84.

1 teaspoon *each* cornstarch, soy sauce, and dry sherry
1 pound chicken breasts, skinned, boned, and cut in bite-size pieces
3½ tablespoons salad oil
2 small zucchini
Cooking sauce (directions follow)
1 clove garlic, minced
1 teaspoon minced fresh ginger
½ cup water chestnuts, cut in quarters
⅓ cup bamboo shoots, cut in ½-inch squares
3 whole green onions, thinly sliced

In a bowl, combine cornstarch, soy, and sherry. Add chicken and stir to coat, then stir in 1½ teaspoons of the oil and let stand for 15 minutes to marinate. Cut each zucchini lengthwise in 4 slices, then cut in ½-inch pieces. Prepare cooking sauce and set aside.

Heat a wok or wide frying pan over high heat. When pan is hot, add 2 tablespoons of the oil. When oil begins to heat, add garlic and ginger. Stir once, then add chicken and stir-fry until chicken is opaque (about 3 minutes). Remove chicken from pan.

Add the remaining 1 tablespoon oil to pan. When oil is hot, add zucchini and stir-fry for 1 minute, adding a few drops water if pan appears dry. Add water chestnuts, bamboo shoots, and onion. Stir-fry for 30 seconds. Return chicken to pan. Stir cooking sauce, pour into pan, and cook, stirring, until sauce bubbles and thickens. Makes 3 or 4 servings.

Cooking sauce. In a bowl, combine 2 teaspoons **cornstarch**, 1 teaspoon *each* **sugar** and **vinegar**, ¼ teaspoon **salt**, 2 tablespoons **hoisin sauce**, 1 tablespoon **soy sauce**, and ¼ cup **chicken broth**.

Once you begin cooking, it takes only five minutes to stir-fry Chicken & Snow Peas (recipe on page 44). You can vary the vegetable to suit your mood and taste.

White Cut Chicken with Spicy Peanut Sauce

Szechwan *(Pictured on page 18)*

Depending on how much lettuce you use, you can serve this as a salad or as part of an appetizer cold plate. The chicken is shredded rather than cut, so the rough edges absorb all of the spicy dressing.

- 1½ pounds chicken breasts
- 1 whole green onion, cut in half
- 1 quarter-size slice fresh ginger, crushed with the side of a cleaver
- 1 tablespoon dry sherry
- ½ teaspoon *each* salt and sugar
- 2 cups water
- 1 to 3 cups shredded iceberg lettuce
  Spicy peanut sauce (directions follow)

Place chicken in a 2-quart pan with the onion, ginger, sherry, salt, sugar, and water. Bring to a boil, cover, and simmer for 20 minutes. Remove from heat and let stand until chicken is cool enough to handle. Strain broth and save for soup. Remove and discard skin from chicken. Pull meat from bones, then pull meat in long shreds. If made ahead, cover and chill.

To serve, mound lettuce on a serving platter. Arrange shredded chicken over lettuce. Drizzle peanut sauce over all. Makes 3 to 6 servings.

Spicy peanut sauce. Stir together 1½ tablespoons creamy **peanut butter** and 2½ tablespoons **salad oil** until blended. Stir in 2 tablespoons *each* **soy sauce** and **sugar**, 2 teaspoons **white vinegar**, ½ teaspoon **sesame oil**, ¼ to ½ teaspoon **ground red pepper** (cayenne) and 1 tablespoon *each* minced **green onion** and **fresh coriander** (also called Chinese parsley or cilantro).

注意 **White cut chicken with sweet sesame sauce.** Follow directions for white cut chicken with spicy peanut sauce, but substitute the following sesame sauce for the spicy peanut sauce. In a wide frying pan over medium heat, toast 2 tablespoons **sesame seeds** (shake pan frequently) until golden (about 2 minutes). Drain the syrup from 1 can (8 oz.) **crushed pineapple**. Mix pineapple with ½ cup canned **plum sauce**, 1½ tablespoons **sugar**, 1 tablespoon **white vinegar**, and the toasted sesame seeds. Pour sauce over chicken and garnish with shredded **green onion** and sprigs of fresh **coriander** (also called Chinese parsley or cilantro).

Chicken Wings with Sweet & Pungent Sauce

(Pictured on page 23)

Chinese cooks prize chicken wings for their silky texture and rich flavor. They generally cook the first and second sections of the wings and save the tips for soup. If you prefer a meatier dish, use only the first sections—they are sold in markets as drummettes.

- 3 pounds chicken wings or drummettes
- 1 tablespoon *each* soy sauce and dry sherry
- ½ teaspoon *each* Chinese five-spice and salt
- 1 clove garlic, crushed with the side of a cleaver
- 1 quarter-size slice fresh ginger, crushed with the side of a cleaver
  Salad oil
- 2 eggs, lightly beaten
  Cornstarch
  Sweet and pungent sauce (directions follow) or hot mustard (page 37) and catsup

Cut chicken wings in sections; save wing tips for broth. In a bowl combine soy, sherry, five-spice, salt, garlic, and ginger. Add chicken and stir to coat. Cover and refrigerate for 1 hour.

In a wide frying pan, pour salad oil to a depth of 1½ inches and heat to 350° on a deep-frying thermometer. Drain chicken and discard garlic and ginger. Dip each piece of chicken in beaten egg, then dredge in cornstarch; shake off excess. Place chicken in hot oil and fry, turning as needed, until crust is golden brown and meat is no longer pink (about 5 to 6 minutes). Remove from pan with a slotted spoon and drain on paper towels. Keep warm in a 200° oven until all wings are cooked. Serve hot with sweet and pungent sauce or hot mustard and catsup. Makes 6 to 8 servings.

Sweet and pungent sauce. In a small pan, heat ¾ cup **water**, ½ cup *each* **sugar** and **vinegar**, 2 tablespoons **catsup**, and 1 tablespoon **soy sauce** until sugar is dissolved. Add ½ cup shredded **mixed sweet pickles** and ¼ teaspoon **sesame oil**. Blend 2 tablespoons *each* **cornstarch** and **water**. Add to pan and cook, stirring, until sauce bubbles and thickens. Serve hot or at room temperature. Makes about 1½ cups sauce.

Phoenix Chicken Rolls with Black Bean Sauce

Canton

Butterflying pieces of chicken breast goes quickly with a sharp knife. You then fill the butterflied chicken pieces with ham and shrimp and roll them into tiny packets to be deep-fried.

If you wish, you can save the chicken bones and skin, to make the chicken broth called for in the black bean sauce.

- 2 large whole chicken breasts
- 10 medium-size raw shrimp, shelled and deveined
- 2 sandwich-size slices cooked ham
  Cornstarch
- 1 cup all-purpose flour, unsifted
- ¼ cup cornstarch
- 1 teaspoon *each* baking powder and salt
- 1¼ cups water
  Salad oil
  Black bean sauce (directions follow)

Split, skin, and bone chicken breasts. Remove the filet, the small piece of meat that lies on top of each side of the breast, then remove the white ligament from each filet.

Cut each side of breast in half lengthwise and crosswise; including the filets, you should have 20 pieces. Cut each piece through the thickness to within ¼ inch of the other side; spread meat open so it forms a rectangle. (Some of the pieces will be slightly irregular in size.)

Cut each shrimp in half crosswise, then hit with the side of a heavy knife blade to mash slightly. Cut ham in matchstick pieces. To make each chicken roll, place ½ shrimp and 1 or 2 strips ham at the short end of each piece of chicken. Roll up to form a cylinder. Coat rolls on all sides with cornstarch, then squeeze gently in your hand to seal. At this point you can cover and refrigerate for as long as 8 hours, but bring to room temperature before cooking in deep fat.

To cook, combine flour, the ¼ cup cornstarch, baking powder, and salt in a bowl. Add water and blend until smooth. In a deep pan, pour 1½ inches salad oil and heat to 360° on a deep-frying thermometer. Dip each chicken roll in batter, drain briefly, then place in hot oil. Fry chicken without crowding, turning occasionally, until crust is golden brown and chicken is opaque (about 3 to 4 minutes). Remove with a slotted spoon, drain on paper towels, then arrange on a heatproof platter. Keep warm in a 200° oven until all rolls are cooked. Pour black bean sauce over chicken just before serving. Makes 20 rolls.

Black bean sauce. Rinse and drain 1 tablespoon **fermented black beans**. Finely chop beans together with 1 large clove **garlic**. In a small pan, heat 1 tablespoon **salad oil** over medium heat. Add bean-garlic mixture and cook, stirring, for 1 minute. Add 1 cup **chicken broth** and 1 tablespoon **dry sherry**. Sim-

mer for 2 minutes. Blend 1 tablespoon **cornstarch** with 1 tablespoon **water**. Add to pan and cook, stirring, until sauce bubbles and thickens slightly (about 1 minute). Stir in ½ teaspoon **sesame oil** and **salt** to taste. If made ahead, reheat sauce before pouring over chicken rolls. Makes 1 cup sauce.

Chicken with Plum Sauce

Canton

Many Chinese recipes for chicken start with deep-frying boneless pieces in a light, crisp batter. What makes this dish distinctive is the flavorful sweet-sour plum sauce laced with strips of pickled ginger.

The lemon sauce that follows is another favorite Cantonese way to create a sweet-sour flavor. The ratio of sugar and lemon varies with the cook, but the final sauce should taste fresh and not overly sweet.

Plum sauce or lemon sauce (directions follow)
1½ pounds chicken breasts or thighs
2 tablespoons soy sauce
1 tablespoon *each* water and cornstarch
¼ teaspoon sesame oil
Dash of white pepper
2 tablespoons salad oil
1 cup all-purpose flour, unsifted
¼ cup cornstarch
1½ teaspoons baking powder
1 cup water
Salad oil

Prepare plum sauce and set aside. Skin and bone chicken; cut in pieces roughly 2 inches square. Pound chicken lightly with the back of a cleaver or heavy knife so each piece is of uniform thickness. In a bowl, combine soy, water, the 1 tablespoon cornstarch, sesame oil, and pepper. Add chicken and stir to coat, then stir in 1 tablespoon of the salad oil and let stand for 15 minutes to marinate.

In a separate bowl, combine flour, the ¼ cup cornstarch, and baking powder. Add the remaining

1 tablespoon salad oil and water and blend until smooth. Let batter stand for 10 minutes.

In a wide frying pan, pour salad oil to a depth of 1½ inches and heat to 350° on a deep-frying thermometer. Dip each piece of chicken in batter, then place in hot oil. Fry chicken without crowding, turning occasionally, until crust is golden brown and meat is no longer pink (about 5 to 6 minutes for breasts, 7 to 8 minutes for thighs). Remove with a slotted spoon and drain on paper towels. Keep warm in a 200° oven until all pieces are cooked. Pass plum sauce to spoon over chicken. Makes 4 or 5 servings.

Plum sauce. In a bowl combine ¾ cup **water**, 1½ teaspoons **cornstarch**, 2 teaspoons **sugar**, 1 teaspoon **soy sauce**, and ¼ cup **canned plum sauce**. In a small pan, heat 1 tablespoon **salad oil** over medium-high heat. Add 2 tablespoons thin-sliced **picked red ginger** and stir-fry for 30 seconds. Pour in plum sauce mixture and cook, stirring, until sauce bubbles and thickens slightly (about 2 minutes). Serve at room temperature. Makes 1 cup sauce.

Lemon sauce. Cut 1 large thin-skinned **lemon** in thin slices; discard any seeds and end pieces. In a small pan, heat 1 tablespoon **salad oil** over medium-high heat. Add lemon slices and stir-fry for 30 seconds. Add 1 cup **chicken broth**, 7 tablespoons **sugar**, 3 tablespoons **lemon juice**, and **salt** to taste. Simmer for 2 minutes. Blend 1 tablespoon **cornstarch** with 1 tablespoon **water**. Pour into sauce and cook, stirring, until sauce bubbles and thickens slightly. Pour over chicken just before serving.

Chinese Chicken Salad

Four hands are faster than two at shredding the chicken for this superb salad, but even without help

you can prepare the ingredients a day ahead, then assemble them just before serving. The result is festive and filling enough to make a company meal with soup and steamed buns (page 87).

- ¼ cup sesame seeds
- ¼ cup all-purpose flour, unsifted
- 1 tablespoon cornmeal
- ½ teaspoon *each* Chinese five-spice and salt
  Dash of pepper
- 2 pounds chicken breasts and thighs
  Salad oil
  Dressing (directions follow)
- ½ medium-size head iceberg lettuce, thinly shredded
- 3 whole green onions, thinly sliced
- 1 small bunch fresh coriander (also called Chinese parsley or cilantro)
- 2 to 3 cups fried bean threads or rice sticks (page 82)

In a wide frying pan over medium heat, toast sesame seeds (shake pan frequently) until golden (about 2 minutes); set aside.

Mix together flour, cornmeal, five-spice, salt, and pepper. Dredge chicken in mixture; shake off excess. Pour oil into pan to a depth of 1½ inches and heat to 375° on a deep-frying thermometer. Add chicken and fry, turning as needed, until well browned on all sides (about 10 minutes for breasts, 12 minutes for thighs). Drain and cool.

If you prefer to oven-fry the chicken after dredging with the flour mixture, arrange in a shallow baking pan. Drizzle with about 2 tablespoons salad oil and bake in a 400° oven for about 50 minutes or until chicken is no longer pink in the thickest part (cut a small gash to test). Turn once, if needed, to brown evenly all over. You can also put the chicken under the broiler briefly to finish browning and crisping the skin.

Use chopsticks to fill lettuce cups with Minced Chicken, then wrap up the package and eat out of hand (recipe on this page). Crisp Egg Rolls (recipe on page 21) and grapes make this a three-star meal.

Meanwhile, prepare dressing and set aside. Skin and bone chicken. This is easier to do if you don't let the chicken become completely cold. Cut the crisp skin in thin slivers. Pull the meat into shreds. At this point you can cover and refrigerate until next day.

To assemble salad, place chicken in a large bowl with lettuce, onion, and coriander. Sprinkle with sesame seeds, drizzle with dressing, and toss. Add bean threads and mix lightly. Makes 4 servings.

Dressing. Combine ½ teaspoon **dry mustard**, 1 teaspoon *each* **sugar** and grated **lemon peel**, 2 teaspoons **soy sauce**, 1 tablespoon **lemon juice**, 1 teaspoon **sesame oil**, and 4 to 6 tablespoons **salad oil**.

Curried Coconut Chicken

Szechwan

Influenced by trade with Burma, the province of Szechwan learned of new seasonings and ingredients and wove them into their local cuisine. Curry, used here with chicken, is one example. This is a good dish to cook ahead, then serve with rice and one or two condiments. Coconut milk is available canned or frozen in many supermarkets.

- 1½ pounds chicken legs and thighs
- 2 teaspoons *each* cornstarch and dry sherry
- 1 teaspoon sugar
- ½ teaspoon salt
  Dash of white pepper
- 2 large white new potatoes
- 1 large onion
- 3 tablespoons salad oil
- 1 to 2 tablespoons curry powder
- ½ teaspoon turmeric
- 1 teaspoon chili powder
- 1 cup chicken broth, page 24 or canned
- ⅔ cup coconut milk
- ½ teaspoon salt
  Condiments: chopped peanuts, green onion, cucumber, and fresh coriander (also called Chinese parsley or cilantro)

Have your meat cutter hack chicken through the bone into 1½-inch pieces; or separate legs and thighs, but leave whole. In a bowl, combine the cornstarch, sherry, sugar, salt, and pepper. Add chicken, stir to coat, and let stand for 15 minutes to marinate. Peel potatoes and cut in 1½-inch chunks. Cut onion in wide wedges.

In a wide frying pan, heat 2 tablespoons of the oil over medium-high heat. Add potato and onion and cook, stirring occasionally, for 5 minutes. Remove vegetables from drippings and set aside. Add the remaining 1 tablespoon oil. When oil is hot, add chicken and cook, turning, until browned on all sides. Push chicken to side of pan. Add curry powder, turmeric, and chili powder to pan juices and cook, stirring, for 30 seconds. Return vegetables to pan. Add chicken broth, coconut milk, and salt. Bring to a boil, reduce heat, cover, and simmer for 30 minutes. Remove cover and continue cooking for 15 minutes or until meat is no longer pink and sauce has thickened slightly. Serve with rice and pass condiments in separate bowls. Makes 4 or 5 servings.

Minced Chicken with Lettuce

(Pictured on opposite page)

This recipe calls for a lot of chopping; if you own a food processor you can use it to mince everything except the chicken. The texture of the meat is best if you cut it first in small pieces and then, using a cleaver or heavy knife, chop it on a cutting board with a steady chop-chop motion. But if you are short on time and are not overly concerned about tradition, you can dice the ingredients into small cubes instead. This dish is too good to pass by. The chicken is coated with a minimum of sauce, so the cold lettuce leaves, which act as a wrapper, remain very crisp.

(Continued on next page)

8 medium-size dried mushrooms
1 teaspoon cornstarch
2 teaspoons *each* dry sherry and water
1 teaspoon soy sauce
½ teaspoon salt
Dash of white pepper
1½ pounds chicken breasts, skinned, boned, and minced
5 tablespoons salad oil
Cooking sauce (directions follow)
1 teaspoon minced fresh ginger
2 cloves garlic, minced
2 green onions (white part only), minced
1 can (about 8 oz.) bamboo shoots, minced
1 can (about 8 oz.) water chestnuts, minced
Hoisin sauce
About 30 iceberg lettuce leaves, washed, drained, and chilled

Cover mushrooms with warm water, let stand for 30 minutes, then drain. Cut off and discard stems; squeeze mushrooms dry, mince, and set aside. In a bowl, combine cornstarch, sherry, water, soy, salt, and pepper. Add chicken and stir to coat, then stir in 1 teaspoon of the oil and let stand for 15 minutes to marinate. Prepare cooking sauce and set aside.

Heat a wok or wide frying pan over high heat. When pan is hot, add 3 tablespoons of the oil. When oil is hot, add chicken and stir-fry until chicken is opaque (about 3 minutes). Set aside.

Add the remaining oil to pan. When oil begins to heat, add ginger, garlic, and onion and stir once. Add mushrooms, bamboo shoots, and water chestnuts and stir-fry for 2 minutes. Return chicken to pan. Stir cooking sauce, add to pan, and cook, stirring, until sauce bubbles and thickens. Serve hot.

To eat, spread a little hoisin sauce on a lettuce leaf, spoon in some chicken, then wrap up in lettuce. Makes 4 to 6 servings.

Cooking sauce. In a bowl, combine 1 teaspoon **soy sauce**, 1 tablespoon **dry sherry**, 2 tablespoons *each* **oyster sauce** and **water**, 1 teaspoon **sesame oil**, ½ teaspoon **sugar**, and 2 teaspoons **cornstarch**.

Chicken & Chinese Sausages

Canton

Chinese sausages, also called *lop cheong*, give a spicy sweetness to this slow-steamed rice and chicken. The sausages are sold both fresh and frozen in Oriental markets. While the chicken-rice dish cooks, you'll have plenty of time to stir-fry a vegetable as an accompaniment.

2 tablespoons *each* soy sauce and dry sherry
1 tablespoon sugar
2 cloves garlic, minced
2 quarter-size slices fresh ginger, crushed with the side of a cleaver
1 pound chicken thighs, boned and cut into 1½-inch square pieces
4 medium-size dried mushrooms
½ pound Chinese sausages
2 tablespoons salad oil
1¾ cups water
1 cup long-grain rice
2 whole green onions, thinly sliced

In a bowl, combine soy, sherry, sugar, garlic, and ginger. Add chicken and stir to coat. Cover and refrigerate for 1 hour. Cover mushrooms with warm water, let stand for 30 minutes, then drain. Cut off and discard stems; squeeze mushrooms dry and thinly slice. Cut sausages in ¼-inch-thick diagonal slices.

Drain chicken, reserving marinade; discard ginger. In a heavy 3-quart pan, heat oil over high heat. Add chicken and cook, turning, until lightly browned (about 2 minutes on each side). Remove chicken and set aside. To the pan, add reserved marinade and water; stir in rice. Bring to a boil over medium-high heat and cook, uncovered, until liquid is absorbed (about 8 to 10 minutes). Reduce heat to low and stir in chicken, sausages, and mushrooms. Cover and simmer, without stirring, until rice is tender (about 45 minutes). To serve, spoon mixture into a serving bowl and sprinkle with green onion. Makes 4 servings.

Western-style Peking Duck

Classic Peking duck is a demanding specialty that even the Chinese limit to restaurant cooking where it is prepared by chefs who rely on long years of experience and special equipment. But there are ways to closely duplicate the same crackling skin and succulent meat at home.

We offer two versions here. In the first, you steam the duck so it sheds much of its fat, then you roast it to brown and crisp the skin. The second method is even less complicated—you roast the duck at a low temperature for a long time.

With either method you can serve Peking duck in the traditional way: Place morsels of the crisp skin and juicy meat on a mandarin pancake, top with green onion slivers and hoisin sauce or plum sauce, and fold the pancake over the filling to eat out of hand. You might present this as part of a Chinese meal or serve it as an hors d'oeuvre.

1 4 to 5-pound duckling
½ teaspoon *each* ground ginger and ground cinnamon
¼ teaspoon *each* ground nutmeg and white pepper
⅛ teaspoon ground cloves
3 tablespoons soy sauce
5 whole green onions
1 tablespoon honey
½ cup hoisin sauce or plum sauce, homemade (directions follow) or purchased
Fresh coriander (also called Chinese parsley or cilantro)
24 mandarin pancakes (page 84)

Rinse duck inside and out and pat dry; cut off tail and discard; reserve giblets for another use.

Mix together ginger, cinnamon, nutmeg, pepper, and cloves. Sprinkle ½ teaspoon of spice mixture inside duck. Stir 1 tablespoon of the soy into remaining spice mixture, then rub evenly over exterior of bird.

Cut one of the green onions in half and tuck inside cavity of duck.

Cover and refrigerate for 2 hours or until next day.

Set duck, breast side up, on a rack over 1½ to 2 inches boiling water. Cover and steam for 1 hour, adding more water, if necessary, as it evaporates. Cool duck so it firms slightly, then drain and discard juices and green onion from cavity.

Set duck, breast side up, on a rack in a baking pan and prick skin all over with a fork. Bake in a 375° oven for 30 minutes. Blend remaining 2 tablespoons soy with honey and brush on duck. Turn oven temperature to 500°. Bake for 5 minutes or until skin becomes richly browned; do not allow skin to char.

While duck is roasting, cut remaining green onions and tops in 1½-inch pieces, then cut lengthwise in thin strips. Serve green onions and hoisin sauce or plum sauce in separate bowls.

When duck is roasted, slice off skin and cut into roughly 2-inch-square pieces. Slice meat into bite-size pieces. Reserve bones for duck soup (page 25). Arrange skin and duck pieces on a serving plate and garnish with coriander.

To eat, put small pieces of skin and meat on a mandarin pancake. Top with a few green onion slivers and a dab of hoisin or plum sauce, then fold pancake around duck and eat with your hands. Makes 4 to 8 servings.

Plum sauce. Beat ½ cup **plum jelly** lightly with a fork; stir in 1½ teaspoons *each* **sugar** and **vinegar** and ¼ cup finely chopped **chutney.** Makes ¾ cup sauce.

注意 **Simplified Peking duck.** Follow directions for western-style Peking duck to wash and rinse duck. Then combine 2 tablespoons **soy sauce** and 1 tablespoon **salad oil**; rub inside and outside of duck. Roll up 2 whole **green onions** and tuck inside cavity of duck with 1 quarter-size slice fresh **ginger.** Pull neck skin down along the back of duck and skewer in place. Set duck, breast side up, on a rack in a baking pan and prick

skin all over with a fork. Bake in a 275° oven for 4 hours. Prick duck several times during roasting to drain more fat. Brush 2 tablespoons **hoisin sauce** on duck. Bake for 10 minutes or until skin becomes richly browned; do not allow skin to char.

Shanghai Duck
(Pictured on page 7)

Red-cooked duck is so tender you can pull the meat from the bone with chopsticks, then eat each succulent bite with steamed buns (page 87)—the traditional accompaniment—or rice. To produce the rich mahogany glaze, the duck needs frequent basting; a bulb baster makes the job easier.

  1 **4 to 5-pound duckling**
  8 **whole green onions**
  2 **cups water**
10 **large dried mushrooms**
 ½ **cup dried lily buds (also called golden needles)**
  3 **tablespoons sugar**
  1 **whole star anise**
 ⅓ **cup soy sauce**
1½ **cups water**
  1 **bunch fresh coriander (also called Chinese parsley or cilantro)**

Rinse duck inside and out and pat dry; cut off tail and discard; reserve giblets for another use. Prick duck on all sides with a fork. In the bottom of a large heavy pan, place 5 of the onions. Set duck, breast side up, on top of onions in pan. Pour in the 2 cups water and bring to a boil; then reduce heat, cover,

and simmer for 1 hour.

Meanwhile, cover mushrooms with warm water, let stand for 30 minutes, then drain. Cut off and discard stems; squeeze mushrooms dry and leave whole. Cover lily buds with warm water, let stand for 30 minutes, then drain. Cut off and discard hard tips of buds, then tie each bud on itself so there is a knot in the middle.

Drain duck and discard the pan juices, cool duck slightly, then rinse inside and out with cold water. Cut 2 green onions in half and tuck inside duck cavity. Place ½ the mushrooms and ½ the lily buds in bottom of the heavy pan. Set duck, breast side up, in pan on top of mushrooms and lily buds. Place remaining mushrooms and lily buds over duck. Twist the remaining green onion into a spiral and secure on top of duck with a toothpick. Sprinkle sugar over duck. Break star anise in pieces and add to pan along with soy and the 1½ cups water. Bring to a boil, then reduce heat, cover, and simmer, basting frequently, until duck is tender and a rich brown (about 2 hours). If done ahead, cool, cover, and refrigerate. Reheat over low heat.

To serve, place most of mushrooms and lily buds on a serving platter. Remove and discard green onions from duck cavity and place duck on mushrooms and lily buds on platter. Tuck coriander inside of cavity. Garnish top of duck with one or two mushrooms and a few lily buds. Skim fat from pan juices and pass separately to pour over duck. Makes 4 to 6 servings.

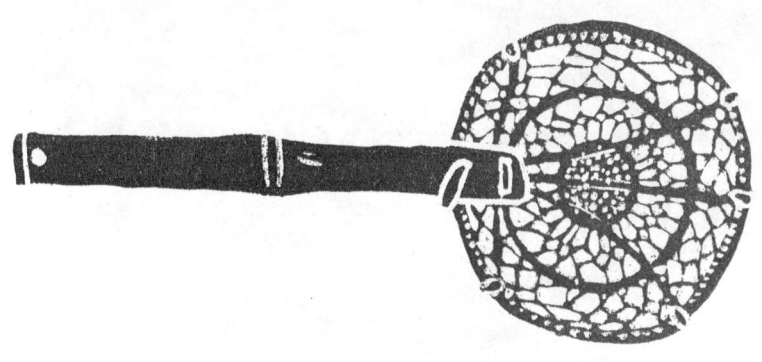

Fish & Shellfish

In cooking, the Chinese are skilled matchmakers—and nowhere is it more evident than in the preparation of seafood. Such unlikely partners as shellfish and pork or fish and bean curd are paired to bring out the best of each, and the marriages produce dishes of infinite variety and superb depth of flavor.

Seasonings as well as ingredients are carefully matched. Ginger, green onion, soy sauce, and sherry are basic. Then the basics are paired with other hot, sweet, spicy, sour, salty, or fragrant flavors.

While the cooking methods found in this chapter are quite simple, you may find some of the eating a challenge, especially if you are accustomed to eating seafood in neat little boneless packages. Fish cooked whole and shellfish cooked in the shell are extremely succulent, and the Chinese feel that the flavor outweighs any effort involved in eating. If you choose to serve seafood this way, you may wish to follow up with another Chinese tradition—pass a basket of small hot cloths for wiping hands at the end of the meal.

Steamed Fish

To the Chinese, a fish without the head and tail looks incomplete. That is one reason they like to cook fish whole. There is little waste, too, when you cook them whole, for you can pick out all the tender nibbles from around the cheeks and tails—considered the choicest morsels—and enjoy picking the skeleton clean.

Unless you catch your own fish or live near an area where seafood is abundant, whole fish may be hard to find. Even Chinese restaurants list their fish specialties on an "available" basis. But you don't need whole fish to enjoy the fine method of steaming fish. What is more important is to use the freshest fish possible—even if the freshest fish comes frozen—and stop the cooking before the fish is overdone.

If you eat fish with chopsticks, you can dip each bite in the delicious sauce before popping it in your mouth. But if you eat this with a fork, you'll want to spoon some of the sauce and garnish over your fish when it is served.

1 or 2 whole fish, 1½ to 2½ lbs. total, such as rockfish, red snapper, or kingfish; or 1½ pounds fish fillets, such as rockfish, turbot, sole, or sea bass
1 to 2 teaspoons salt
3 quarter-size slices fresh ginger
4 whole green onions
2 to 3 tablespoons salad oil
5 sprigs fresh coriander (also called Chinese parsley or cilantro)
2 tablespoons matchstick pieces fresh ginger
2 tablespoons soy sauce

Clean and scale whole fish. Make 3 diagonal slices across body on each side of fish. Rub fish inside and out with 2 teaspoons salt. If you use fillets, rub 1 teaspoon salt on all sides. Place on a heatproof dish or platter that will fit inside a

Choose the freshest fish in the market for this delicious and classic Steamed Fish with Clams (recipe on page 56).

steamer. Place the 3 ginger slices on fish.

Cut 2 of the onions in 1½-inch lengths and place on fish. (If done ahead, cover, and refrigerate up to 4 hours, but bring fish to room temperature before steaming.) Cut the other 2 onions in 1½-inch lengths, then slice lengthwise in thin shreds; reserve.

Place dish on rack in steamer. Cover and steam over boiling water until fish flakes when prodded in thickest part with a fork (8 to 10 minutes for small fish or fillets, 10 to 12 minutes for a 1½ pound fish, 16 to 18 minutes for a 2½ pound fish). While fish is steaming, heat oil in a small pan until hot but not smoking.

Remove dish with fish from steamer, discard ginger and green onion, and tip dish slightly to drain off cooking liquid. Sprinkle onion shreds, coriander, ginger, and soy over fish. Pour hot oil over fish just before serving. For easy serving, slide a second dish of the same size under the hot one before bringing to the table. Makes 3 to 6 servings.

注意 **Steamed fish with clams.** (Pictured on page 55) With a brush, scrub about 1 dozen small clams in the shell. Follow directions for steamed fish, but arrange clams on dish around fish just before steaming. Cook clams until the shells open (about 8 minutes). If you steam a large fish which requires longer cooking, remove clams after they open, then return them to the serving dish after you have drained the cooking liquid from the fish.

Szechwan Fish Rolls

Mellow-flavored fish rolls make a delicous and unusual first course or light luncheon entrée. If you wish to include this as part of a Szechwan-style dinner, serve it first, then follow with the more spicy dishes. The components—wrappers, filling, and sauce—can all be made a day ahead.

Egg wrappers (directions follow)
1 pound boneless sole fillets
1 whole green onion, finely chopped
1 tablespoon minced fresh ginger
½ teaspoon salt
⅛ teaspoon white pepper
2 tablespoons salad oil
1 tablespoon *each* sesame oil, dry sherry, and cornstarch
1 egg, separated
  Green onion sauce (directions follow)

If made ahead and refrigerated, let wrappers reach room temperature (they tear when cold). Cut fish into ¼ by 1-inch pieces; combine in a bowl with onion, ginger, salt, pepper, salad oil, sesame oil, sherry, and cornstarch. Beat egg white and stir into fish mixture. Beat egg yolk lightly and reserve.

To assemble, lay egg wrapper wedges, lighter side up, on a board. Place 1 tablespoon of fish mixture in center and dot corners with egg yolk. Starting at wide end, roll wrapper one-third of the way, tuck sides in around filling, then continue rolling toward point of wrapper. Repeat until all wrappers are filled. Arrange fish rolls in two lightly greased 9-inch pie pans.

To cook, drape wax paper over tops of rolls. Place 1 pan on rack in steamer, cover, and steam over boiling water for 10 minutes. Remove pan, cover with foil, and keep in a warm oven while you steam second pan of fish rolls. To serve, arrange steamed rolls on a large platter or individual plates and pour over green onion sauce. Makes 28 rolls, enough to serve 4 as an entrée, or 6 to 8 as a first course.

Egg wrappers. Whirl 7 **eggs,** 1 tablespoon *each* **water** and **salad oil** or sesame oil, ¼ teaspoon **salt,** ⅛ teaspoon **white pepper,** and 1 teaspoon **cornstarch** in a blender until smooth. You should have about 1¾ cups.

Heat a 12-inch frying pan over medium heat; add ½ teaspoon **butter** or margarine and swirl to coat pan bottom. Pour in ¼ cup egg mixture and tilt pan to coat bottom evenly. Let cook until top

is dry but bottom has not quite started to brown (about 20 seconds). Remove from pan. Repeat, using ½ teaspoon butter and ¼ cup batter for each wrapper; you should have 7 round wrappers. Cut each wrapper in quarters to make 4 wedges each. If made ahead, cover and refrigerate.

Green onion sauce. In a small pan, combine 1½ cups **chicken broth** (page 24 or canned), 1½ tablespoons **dry sherry,** 1 tablespoon **salad oil,** 1 teaspoon **sesame oil,** 1 tablespoon **cornstarch** mixed with 1 tablespoon **water,** dash of **white pepper,** and **salt** to taste. Cook, stirring, over high heat until sauce bubbles and thickens slightly; stir in ½ cup **sliced green onion.**

Steamed Fish with Bean Curd

You get more mileage from a pound of fish when you combine it with creamy cubes of bean curd glazed with a flavorful bean sauce. The juices that form during cooking are good to spoon over rice.

½ pound bean curd or tofu
2 tablespoons bean sauce
1 tablespoon dry sherry
1 teaspoon sugar
½ teaspoon salt
1 pound fish fillets, such as rockfish, turbot, sole, or sea bass
2 quarter-size slices fresh ginger
1 whole green onion
2 tablespoons salad oil
3 sprigs fresh coriander (also called Chinese parsley or cilantro)

Place bean curd in a colander and let drain for 15 minutes. Cut in 1-inch cubes, then place between paper towels and gently press out excess water. Combine bean sauce, sherry, sugar, and salt. Rub 1 tablespoon of the mixture on all sides of the fish. Place fish in a single layer in a shallow heatproof bowl. Place ginger on fish. Scatter bean curd on top of fish, then drizzle over remaining bean sauce mixture. Cut onion in 1½-inch lengths, then slice lengthwise in thin shreds; reserve.

To cook, drape wax paper over top of bowl. Place bowl on rack in steamer. Cover and steam over boiling water until fish flakes when prodded in thickest part with a fork (about 8 to 10 minutes). While fish is steaming, heat oil in a small pan until hot but not smoking.

Remove bowl with fish from steamer and discard ginger. Sprinkle onion and coriander over fish. Pour hot oil slowly over fish (it will splatter when it hits the cooking juices) and serve at once. Makes 4 or 5 servings.

Fish Fillets in Wine Sauce

Peking

Since the sauce here is made separately, you can prepare it ahead of time, then thicken it with cornstarch while the fish quickly cooks.

- 4   large dried mushrooms
- ¾   cup chicken broth, page 24 or canned
- 2   tablespoons dry sherry
- 1   teaspoon sugar
- 2   teaspoons soy sauce
- 1   egg
- ½   teaspoon salt
- ⅛   teaspoon white pepper
- 1   pound fish fillets, such as rockfish, turbot, sole, or sea bass, cut in 2-inch squares
  Cornstarch
- 2   tablespoons salad oil
- 2   teaspoons *each* cornstarch and water, combined
- 1   teaspoon sesame oil

Cover mushrooms with warm water, let stand for 30 minutes, then pour off ¼ cup of soaking liquid and place in a small pan; discard remaining liquid.

Cut off and discard stems; slice mushrooms. Place mushrooms in pan with soaking liquid; add chicken broth, sherry, sugar, and soy. Bring to a boil; reduce heat, cover, and simmer until mushrooms are tender (about 20 minutes).

Beat egg with salt and pepper. Dip pieces of fish in egg, then coat lightly with cornstarch. In a wide frying pan, heat salad oil over medium-high heat. Add fish and cook until it flakes when prodded in thickest part with a fork (about 3 minutes per side).

Stir cornstarch and water. Add to sauce and cook, stirring, until sauce bubbles and thickens. Stir in sesame oil. Transfer fish to a serving platter; pour sauce over fish before serving. Makes 3 or 4 servings.

Swimming Sweet & Sour Fish

Whimsy and artistry blend in this handsome and flavorful Chinese fish dish. Carp swimming in the Yellow River in China inspired the original version. In this version, trout from our waters take the place of carp.

  Sweet and sour vegetable sauce (directions follow)
- 4   (about 2 to 3 lbs.) whole trout
- 3   tablespoons dry sherry
- 1   teaspoon soy sauce
  Salt
  About 1/3 cup cornstarch
  Salad oil

Prepare sweet and sour vegetable sauce and set aside. Clean fish, rinse, and dry with paper towels. Mix sherry and soy and brush over surface and cavity of each fish; sprinkle lightly with salt. Lightly coat outside of fish with cornstarch; shake off excess.

In a wide frying pan, pour salad oil to a depth of ½ inch and heat to 360° on a deep-frying thermometer. Cook fish, without crowding, until skin is crusty and fish flakes in thickest part when prodded with a fork (about 2 to 3 minutes on a side). Unlike a flour coating, cornstarch will become crusty, but not brown. Drain on paper towels. If all the fish won't fit in the pan at once, cook in two batches. Keep fish warm while you finish the sauce.

With a slotted spoon, ladle vegetables from sauce onto a large heated platter. To simulate rippling water, use the prongs of a fork to guide vegetables into parallel lines. Place hot trout on vegetables, then pour remaining sauce over fish. Serve at once. Makes 4 servings.

Sweet and sour vegetable sauce. In a small pan, blend ⅓ cup **sugar** (half white and half brown), 1½ tablespoons **cornstarch,** ⅓ cup **white vinegar,** ¾ cup **chicken broth,** 2 teaspoons **soy sauce,** and 2 tablespoons **dry sherry.** Add 1½ teaspoons minced **fresh ginger,** 1 clove **garlic** (minced), 1 small **carrot** (cut in matchstick pieces), and ½ cup sliced **bamboo shoots** (cut in matchstick pieces). Stirring, bring to a boil; reduce heat, cover, and simmer until carrot is crisp-tender (about 5 minutes). Keep warm while you fry the fish. Have ready 1 small **green pepper** (seeded and cut in matchstick pieces) and 3 whole **green onions** (cut in 2-inch lengths). To serve, add pepper and onion to sauce, bring to a boil, and use at once.

Crab in Black Bean Sauce

Canton

If you are unfamiliar with fermented black beans, don't let their pungent odor stop you in your tracks. When a spoonful of the small soft beans are cooked with garlic and ginger, they create a flavor that is appealing to even the most conservative taste.

Oriental markets sell the beans in small plastic bags. Tightly covered, they'll keep almost indefinitely at cool room temperature or in the refrigerator. Since the beans are salted, they should be placed in a sieve and rinsed before using.

Cantonese cooks use black beans to flavor many dishes. This mellow crab dish is one of their favorites. It is messy to eat, but well worth the effort.

(Continued on page 59)

1 **large cooked crab (1½ to 2 lbs.),** cleaned and cracked
3 **tablespoons salad oil**
1½ **tablespoons fermented black beans, rinsed, drained, and finely chopped**
1 **large clove garlic, minced**
¾ **teaspoon minced fresh ginger**
1 **small green pepper, seeded and cut in 1-inch squares**
1 **tablespoon** *each* **soy sauce and dry sherry**
2 **whole green onions, cut in 1-inch lengths**
⅓ **cup chicken broth**

Cut crab body in quarters; leave legs and claws whole.

Heat a wok or wide frying pan over high heat. When pan is hot, add oil. When oil begins to heat, add black beans, garlic, and ginger. Stir-fry for 5 seconds. Add green pepper and stir-fry for 1 minute. Add crab, soy, sherry, onion, and chicken broth. Cook, stirring, until crab is hot (about 3 minutes). Makes 3 or 4 servings.

Crab Curry

Canton   (Pictured on page 63)

It's hard to stop eating this dish once you get your fingers covered with sauce. You may want to pass a basket of hot damp cloths at the table when the last bite is gone.

Cooking sauce (directions follow)
1 **teaspoon** *each* **salt and sugar**
4 **teaspoons curry powder**
¼ **pound boneless lean pork, finely chopped or ground**
1 **large cooked crab (1½ to 2 pounds), cleaned and cracked**
3 **tablespoons salad oil**
1 **large clove garlic, minced**
1 **medium-size onion, cut in wedges with layers separated**
1 **medium-size green pepper, seeded and cut in 1-inch squares**
1 **egg, lightly beaten**

For individual servings, cook Pan-fried Noodles (recipe on page 81) in small cakes, then top with Stir-fried Squid & Peas (recipe on page 62).

Prepare cooking sauce and set aside. Sprinkle salt, sugar, and curry powder over pork; mix well. Cut crab body in quarters; leave legs and claws whole.

Heat a wok or wide frying pan over high heat. When pan is hot, add oil. When oil begins to heat, add garlic. Stir once around pan, then add pork and stir-fry until pork loses its pinkness (about 2 minutes). Add onion and green pepper to pork and stir-fry for 1 minute. Add crab and cook until heated through (about 3 minutes). Add cooking sauce, and cook, stirring, until sauce bubbles and thickens. Stir in egg just until egg begins to set (about 30 seconds). Makes 3 or 4 servings.

Cooking sauce. In a bowl, combine ¾ cup **chicken broth** and 1 table-spoon *each* **cornstarch, soy sauce,** and **dry sherry.**

注意 **Shrimp curry.** Follow directions for crab curry, but use 1 pound medium-size raw **shrimp** (shelled and deveined) in place of crab. Add shrimp to stir-fried pork-vegetable mixture; stir-fry until shrimp turn pink (about 3 minutes); then add cooking sauce.

Phoenix-tail Shrimp

A puffed, crunchy batter coats shrimp in this simply prepared dish. Serve it as a main course or appetizer with your choice of a dipping sauce. Hot mustard and catsup or the sweet and sour sauce mark the dish Cantonese. The salt-pepper mix suggests Peking.

1 **pound medium-size or large raw shrimp**
1 **cup unsifted all-purpose flour**
2½ **teaspoons baking powder**
¼ **teaspoon salt**
Dash of white pepper
1 **cup water**
Salad oil
Dipping sauces: catsup and hot mustard, or sweet and sour kumquat sauce (page 40), or salt-pepper mix (page 37)

Shell shrimp, but leave the tail sections on for handles. Devein, wash, and pat dry with paper towels. In a bowl, combine flour, baking powder, salt, and pepper. Add water and stir until batter is smooth.

In a deep pan, pour oil to a depth of 1½ inches and heat to 375° on a deep-frying thermometer. Holding shrimp by the tail, dip into batter so it covers shrimp but not the tail, then lower into hot oil. Cook several pieces at a time without crowding, turning occasionally, until crisp and light golden (about 2 to 3 minutes). Remove with a slotted spoon and drain on paper towels. Serve with dipping sauce of your choice. Makes 4 servings.

Szechwan Shrimp

Cooked in their shells, these spicy shrimp are incredibly tender. Yet, because you cut the shells open to devein the shrimp before cooking, they are easy to eat with chopsticks.

1 **pound medium-size or large raw shrimp**
1 **tablespoon salt**
Cooking sauce (directions follow)
2½ **tablespoons salad oil**
3 **large cloves garlic, minced**
1 **teaspoon minced fresh ginger**
¼ **teaspoon crushed red pepper**
4 **whole green onions, thinly sliced**

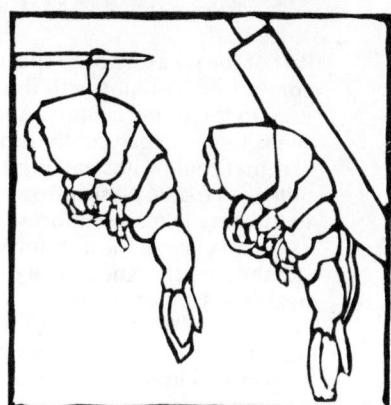

To devein raw shrimp, insert a toothpick beneath sand vein and lift out vein; or slit back open with a knife and remove vein.

(Continued on next page)

Cut shrimp through back of shell with scissors and devein. Place shrimp in a bowl and sprinkle with salt. With your hands, rub salt into shrimp. Let stand for 15 minutes, then rinse well, drain, and pat dry with paper towels.

Prepare the cooking sauce and set aside.

Heat a wok or wide frying pan over medium heat. When pan is hot, add 1½ tablespoons of the oil. When oil is hot, add shrimp and stir-fry until the shells turn pink and shrimp are opaque throughout (about 3 to 4 minutes). Remove from pan.

Heat the remaining 1 tablespoon oil. Add garlic, ginger, and red pepper and stir-fry for 5 seconds. Return shrimp to pan, add green onion, and stir once. Stir cooking sauce, add to pan, and cook, stirring, until sauce bubbles and thickens. Makes 3 or 4 servings.

Cooking sauce. In a bowl, combine 1 tablespoon *each* **Worcestershire** and **dry sherry**, 2 tablespoons **catsup**, ¼ cup **water**, 2 teaspoons **sugar**, ½ teaspoon **salt**, and 1½ teaspoons **cornstarch.**

Hot & Sour Shrimp

Szechwan

Not all food from Szechwan is searingly hot. Here shrimp are moderately seasoned with chile pepper; the pungency comes from garlic and ginger.

 1 **pound medium-size raw shrimp, shelled and deveined**
 1 **tablespoon dry sherry**
   Cooking sauce (directions follow)
 3 **tablespoons salad oil**
 3 **cloves garlic, minced**
 1½ **tablespoons minced fresh ginger**
 ¼ **teaspoon crushed red pepper**
 2 **large stalks celery, cut in ½-inch-thick slices**
 ½ **cup sliced bamboo shoots**
 2 **whole green onions, thinly sliced**

Toss shrimp with sherry. Prepare cooking sauce and set aside.

Heat a wok or wide frying pan over high heat. When pan is hot, add 1½ tablespoons of the oil. When oil begins to heat, add garlic, ginger, and red pepper. Stir once, add shrimp, and stir-fry until they turn pink (about 3 minutes). Remove from pan.

Heat the remaining 1½ tablespoons oil. Add celery and bamboo shoots and stir-fry for 1 minute. Stir cooking sauce, then add to pan along with shrimp and green onion. Cook, stirring, until sauce bubbles and thickens. Makes 3 or 4 servings.

Cooking sauce. In a small bowl, combine ¼ cup **vinegar**, 2 tablespoons **soy sauce**, 5 teaspoons **sugar**, and 2 teaspoons **cornstarch.**

Cold Spiced Shrimp

A delicious make-ahead dish, these shrimp are an easy addition to a multi-course Chinese meal. They are also good as part of an appetizer cold plate. The aromatic Szechwan peppercorns provide the haunting pungency.

 ½ **pound medium-size or large raw shrimp**
 1 **tablespoon minced fresh ginger**
 4 **whole green onions, finely chopped**
 1 **tablespoon dry sherry**
 1 **teaspoon salt**
 1 **teaspoon Szechwan peppercorns or whole black peppers**
   About 1¼ cups water

# Clay pot cooking

Part of the pleasure of preparing ethnic food comes from cooking with the same equipment used in the home country. About 3000 years ago, the Chinese began cooking in pots made from clay that could withstand high temperatures. Still used today, these inexpensive pots can be found here in many import shops.

At first glance, the pots look like ovenware, but they are designed to be used over direct heat. The Chinese use them for casserole cooking and long-cooking soups and stews; but they also use them to prepare just one step in a recipe. Many cooks believe that food cooked in clay has a purer, sweeter, more mellow flavor. Because of their rustic good looks, you can cook and serve in the same pot—the clay keeps food so hot that it comes to the table sizzling in its juices. Or you can simply use the pots as handsome serving containers at the table.

With their slightly rough, bisque-colored exteriors and dark, glazed interiors, clay pots are easy to spot. You will find them in photographs throughout this book. Some have lids (glazed or unglazed) with a wire handle or clay knob. Some are encased in wire to help prevent breakage and to conduct heat more evenly.

Before using a clay pot, soak it (and lid, if it has one) in water for at least 24 hours, drain, then let dry for another 24 hours. No further soaking is necessary. Avoid extreme changes in temperature when using the pot. Place a wire diffuser over electric elements; with gas, set the pot directly on the burner. Do not set a chilled clay pot directly on a hot burner—or place a heated pot on a cold or wet surface or fill it with cold water. Wash the glazed interior of the pot gently with water and a mild detergent; do not scratch.

Wash unshelled shrimp, then place in a small pan. Add ginger, onion, sherry, salt, and peppercorns. Barely cover with water. Bring to simmering, then cover and simmer just until shrimp turn pink (about 3 to 4 minutes). Chill shrimp in stock, then shell and devein. Return to stock, cover, and chill. Drain stock before serving. Makes 3 to 6 servings.

Gingered Oysters

If you wish to serve this sauced dish with rice, start the rice cooking first, because it takes less than 15 minutes to prepare and cook the oysters.

- 1 jar (about 10 oz.) fresh oysters, drained
- ⅛ teaspoon Chinese five-spice
- 1½ teaspoons cornstarch
- 4 teaspoons soy sauce
- 1½ tablespoons *each* dry sherry and water
- 10 whole green onions
- 2 tablespoons salad oil
- 4 dime-size slices peeled fresh ginger

If oysters are large, cut into bite-size pieces. In a bowl, blend five-spice and 1 teaspoon each of the cornstarch and soy. Add oysters and stir to coat; let stand for 10 minutes. Blend the remaining cornstarch and soy with sherry and water; set aside. Cut green onions in half lengthwise, then cut in 1½-inch lengths.

Heat a wok or wide frying pan over medium-high heat. When pan is hot, add 1 tablespoon of the oil. When oil begins to heat, add ginger and stir-fry for 10 seconds. Add green onion and stir-fry for 30 seconds. Remove from pan.

Reduce heat to medium. Add the remaining 1 tablespoon oil. When oil is hot, add oysters and stir-fry until oysters are firmed slightly (about 2 minutes). Return ginger and green onion to pan. Stir cornstarch mixture to recombine. Add to pan and cook, stirring, until sauce bubbles and thickens. Makes 2 or 3 servings.

Lobster Cantonese

Although the popular name for the sauce in this recipe is lobster sauce, it actually contains no lobster. It gained its name because it is traditionally used in combination with lobster; but the flavor is superb with crab, shrimp, and scallops, too. Adding the egg gives the sauce a silky finish.

Chinese cooks feel that shellfish are more succulent when they are sheathed in their protective shells, but for easier eating, you may wish to remove the shells before cooking. If you cook crab, however, do not shell, as the meat would disintegrate during the stir-frying.

Cooking sauce (directions follow)
- 1½ pounds raw lobster tails (thaw, if frozen)
- 3 tablespoons salad oil
- 2 tablespoons fermented black beans, rinsed, drained, and finely chopped
- 2 cloves garlic, finely chopped
- 1 teaspoon minced fresh ginger
- ¼ pound boneless lean pork, finely chopped or ground
- 1 whole green onion, thinly sliced
- 1 egg, lightly beaten

Prepare cooking sauce and set aside. If you want to cook the lobster in the shell, trim side fins. Cut tails in half lengthwise and devein; if large, cut in half crosswise. Or remove meat from the shell and cut in bite-size pieces.

Heat a wok or wide frying pan over high heat. When pan is hot, add oil. When oil begins to heat, add beans, garlic, and ginger. Stir once, then add pork and stir-fry until it loses its pinkness (about 2 minutes).

Add lobster and cook, stirring constantly, until the shells turn red or, if shelled, the meat is opaque throughout (about 3 to 4 minutes). Stir cooking sauce, add to pan, and cook, stirring, until sauce bubbles and thickens. Add onion and egg; stir just until egg begins to set (about 30 seconds). Makes 3 or 4 servings.

Cooking sauce. Stir together 1 tablespoon *each* **cornstarch, soy sauce,** and **dry sherry;** ½ cup **chicken broth;** and dash of **white pepper.**

注意 **Crab Cantonese.** Follow directions for lobster Cantonese, but use 1 large cooked **crab** (1½ to 2 pounds), cleaned and cracked, in place of lobster. Cut body in quarters; leave legs and claws whole. Cook crab until it is heated through (about 3 to 4 minutes).

注意 **Shrimp Cantonese.** Follow directions for lobster Cantonese, but use 1 pound medium-size raw **shrimp** in place of lobster. Cut through back of shell with scissors and devein, or remove shells and devein. Cook shrimp until they turn pink (about 3 minutes).

注意 **Scallops Cantonese.** Follow directions for lobster Cantonese, but use 1 pound **scallops** in place of lobster. Cut in ¼-inch thick slices. Cook scallops until they are opaque throughout (about 3 minutes).

Stir-fried Squid & Peas

(Pictured on page 58)

Like abalone, squid becomes tough when overcooked. Chinese cooks eliminate this problem by scoring the squid first. The crosshatch design is not only decorative but permits rapid cooking. In this recipe, the tender pieces of squid cooked without a batter, become tinged with royal splashes of purple.

- 1 pound squid
- 2 tablespoons salad oil
- ½ teaspoon minced fresh ginger
- 1 cup frozen peas, thawed
- ½ cup chicken broth
- 1 teaspoon soy sauce
- 1 tablespoon oyster sauce
- ¼ teaspoon sugar
- 2 teaspoons cornstarch
- 1 tablespoon water

Clean squid by following the illustrations below. **1.** Peel off and discard transparent speckled membrane from the hood, exposing the white meat of the hood. **2.** Pull out the long transparent, sword-shaped shell from inside the hood and discard it. **3.** Holding the hood in one hand and body (with tentacles) in the other, pull gently on body to separate it from hood. Strip off and discard any material that separates easily from the body, including the ink sac. If ink sac breaks, rinse body to remove ink. Squeeze out and discard contents of hood; rinse inside. **4.** Turn body upside down so tentacles are spread open. Squeeze gently to pop out the hard, parrotlike beak from between the tentacles. **5.** Slit hood lengthwise and open flat. With a knife, make ½-inch-wide diagonal cuts across the inside of the hood. Repeat in opposite direction so knife marks look like crosshatching. Cut hood in roughly 2-inch square pieces. Wash squares and tentacles, drain, and pat dry.

Heat a wok or wide frying pan over medium high heat. When pan is hot, add 1 tablespoon of the oil. When oil begins to heat, add ginger and stir once. Add squid and stir-fry just until the edges curl (about 1½ to 2 minutes). Remove from pan.

Heat the remaining 1 tablespoon oil. Add peas and stir-fry for 1 minute. Add chicken broth, soy, oyster sauce, and sugar, and bring to a boil. Cook peas for 1 minute. Blend cornstarch and water. Add to pan, and cook, stirring, until sauce bubbles and thickens. Return squid to pan, stir, then serve at once. Makes 3 or 4 servings.

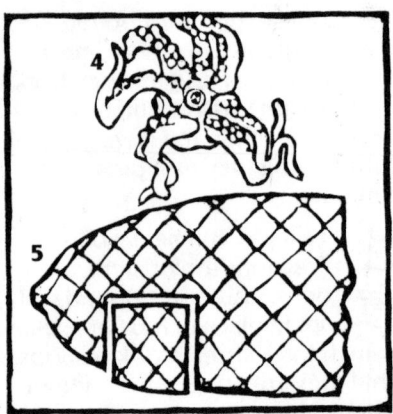

Sizzling Sweet & Sour Seafood

You don't need to plan another starch when you serve this seafood combination over crisp rice cakes. Organize the cooking with the final assembly in mind—in order to create the sizzling sound, both rice cakes and topping must be hot.

- Cooking sauce (directions follow)
- 3 tablespoons salad oil
- 2 cloves garlic, minced
- 1 teaspoon minced fresh ginger
- ½ pound medium-size raw shrimp, shelled and deveined
- ½ pound scallops, halved
- 1 carrot, very thinly sliced
- ½ cup sliced bamboo shoots
- 1 green pepper, seeded and cut in 1-inch squares
- 5 whole green onions, cut in 1½-inch lengths
- ¼ teaspoon salt
- 6 2-inch squares sizzling rice (page 81)

Prepare cooking sauce and set aside. Heat wok or wide frying pan over high heat. When pan is hot, add 1½ tablespoons of the oil. When oil begins to heat, add garlic and ginger. Stir once, then add shrimp and scallops and stir-fry until shrimp turn pink and scallops are opaque throughout (about 3 minutes). Remove from pan and set aside.

Heat the remaining 1½ tablespoons oil in pan. Add carrot and bamboo shoots and stir-fry for 3 minutes, adding a few drops water if pan apppears dry. Add pepper, onion, and salt and stir-fry for 1 minute. Return shrimp and scallops to pan. Stir cooking sauce, pour into pan, and cook, stirring, until sauce bubbles and thickens.

Turn off heat, cover, and keep hot while you fry sizzling rice as directed on page 81. Turn seafood mixture into a preheated bowl. Bring hot fried rice cakes to the table on a platter and immediately pour over seafood mixture. Makes 3 or 4 servings.

Cooking sauce. In a bowl, combine ⅓ cup *each* **sugar, white wine vinegar,** and **chicken broth;** 2 tablespoons **soy sauce;** 1 tablespoon **dry sherry;** and 1½ tablespoons **cornstarch.**

Use fingers, not forks, to fully enjoy Crab Curry (recipe on page 59); when the last bite is gone, pass a basket of damp cloths.

Bean Curd & Eggs

The Chinese are very partial to both bean curd and eggs. If you explore a Chinese market, you can see bean curd in creamy white blocks, golden brown fried puffs, and dried leathery sheets. Eggs are displayed in myriad sizes and colors, from crates of tiny speckled quail eggs to duck eggs with the look of alabaster; from tawny brown hen's eggs to black-coated thousand-year-old eggs buried in an ash and lime mixture in dragon-decorated pots. (In reality, these preserved eggs are only 100 days old and are eaten as an appetizer.)

As you might guess, bean curd and eggs are essential ingredients for a variety of meatless and almost meatless dishes. In this chapter we take a look at ways you can duplicate the Chinese flavor by using bean curd and eggs from your own market.

Fish-stuffed Bean Curd

(Pictured on page 70)

One popular way to prepare bean curd is to stuff it with a savory mixture and fry it to develop a full-bodied flavor and tender meaty texture. You can prepare most of this dish in advance, then reheat it in broth and serve it with rice.

- 1 package (about 1 lb. 6 oz.) bean curd or tofu
  Fish stuffing (directions follow)
  Salad oil
- 3 cloves garlic, minced
- ½ head iceberg lettuce, cut in 2-inch squares
- ¼ cup frozen peas, thawed
- 1 can (4 oz.) whole mushrooms, drained
- 1 cup chicken broth, page 24 or canned
- 1 tablespoon cornstarch
- 2 tablespoons soy sauce or oyster sauce
- 1 tablespoon water

Cut bean curd squares in half diagonally to make 8 triangles. If you use tofu, cut the block crosswise in 4 equal slices, then cut each slice in half diagonally. Place in a colander and let drain for 15 minutes, then place between paper towels and gently press out excess water. If you use tofu, change paper towels several times until they no longer soak up any moisture.

On widest side of each triangle, cut a pocket to within ½ inch of edges. Gently stuff each pocket with about 1½ teaspoons fish filling.

In a wok or deep pan, pour oil to a depth of about 1½ inches and heat to 350° on a deep-frying thermometer. Add several bean curd triangles at a time and fry, turning once, until golden on all sides (about 4 to 5 minutes). Remove from oil and drain on paper towels. Cool, cover, and chill, if made ahead.

In a wide frying pan or Chinese clay pot (1 quart or larger) that can be used on top of range, heat 1 tablespoon salad oil over medium-high heat. Add garlic and cook, stirring, just until it begins to brown. Add lettuce, then stir and cook just until lettuce begins to wilt (about 1 minute). Stir in peas and mushrooms; top with stuffed bean curd. Pour broth over bean curd, cover, and simmer over low heat for 8 minutes (15 minutes if chilled).

Stir together cornstarch, soy, and water. Push bean curd away from one side of pan and stir soy mixture into broth; cook, stirring carefully so as not to break bean curd, until sauce bubbles and thickens. Makes 2 or 3 servings.

Fish stuffing. Finely chop ¼ pound boneless lean **white fish fillets** (such as rockfish or turbot). Mix fish with 2 teaspoons minced **green onion**; 1 teaspoon **soy sauce**; ¼ teaspoon *each* **cornstarch, salad oil,** and **sesame oil**; ⅛ teaspoon *each* **salt, sugar,** and **liquid hot pepper seasoning;** and a dash of **pepper.**

Bean Curd & Peanut Salad

Shanghai

This is not a salad in the Western sense, but a cool combination to serve as a side dish in a Chinese meal or to feature at a summer picnic. Baking the bean curd first eliminates excess moisture, so the curd keeps its shape when sliced and tossed.

> About ⅔ **pound bean curd or tofu**
> **Salad oil**
> ½ **pound bean sprouts**
> 1 **small cucumber**
> 3 **tablespoons white wine vinegar**
> 1½ **tablespoons** *each* **sugar and salad oil**
> 1 **teaspoon sesame oil**
> ½ **teaspoon salt**
> ⅛ **teaspoon ground red pepper (cayenne)**
> 2 **whole green onions, thinly sliced**
> ½ **small carrot, shredded**
> ½ **cup salted peanuts, coarsely chopped**

Cut bean curd in 1-inch-thick slices. Place in a colander and let drain for 15 minutes, then place between paper towels and gently press out excess water. Place slices on a rack set in a shallow-rimmed baking pan. Brush all surfaces with salad oil. Bake in a 350° oven for 20 minutes. Cut bean curd in ¼ by ¼ by 1-inch strips; chill.

Cook bean sprouts in a large pot of boiling water for 30 seconds. Drain, rinse with cold water, and drain again; chill. Peel cucumber, leaving alternating strips of green for color. Cut in half lengthwise and scoop out seeds if large; thinly slice and chill. Mix together vinegar, sugar, salad oil, sesame oil, salt, and red pepper.

Just before serving, combine bean curd, bean sprouts, cucumber, green onion, carrot, and peanuts. Pour dressing over all and toss lightly. Makes 4 or 5 servings.

Bean Curd with Vegetables

In this savory meatless dish, you combine broccoli, green beans, or carrots with silky slices of bean curd. Oyster sauce gives a rich depth to the gravy. Because bean curd is tender and breaks easily, you may find it easiest to cook this dish in a wide frying pan that will give you ample surface for browning and turning the slices.

> About 1 **pound bean curd or tofu**
> ½ **teaspoon salt**
> **Cooking sauce (directions follow)**
> 1 **pound broccoli, green beans, or carrots**
> 1 **teaspoon** *each* **salt and sugar**
> 2 **quarter-size slices fresh ginger, crushed with the side of a cleaver**
> 1 **tablespoon** *each* **salad oil and dry sherry**
> 4 **tablespoons salad oil**
> ¼ **pound mushrooms, quartered**
> 1 **tablespoon dry sherry**
> ½ **teaspoon sugar**

Place bean curd in a colander and let drain for 15 minutes. Cut in

domino-shaped pieces, then place between paper towels and gently press out excess water. Sprinkle with the ½ teaspoon salt and set aside. Prepare cooking sauce and set aside.

If you use broccoli, cut off flowerets, cut them in half if large, and slash the stems. Peel thick stalks and thinly slice. If you use green beans, remove ends and strings; cut in 2-inch-long slanting slices. If you use carrots, peel and cut in ¼-inch-thick slanting slices. Place 4 cups water, salt, sugar, ginger, and the 1 tablespoon each oil and sherry in a 3-quart pan. Bring water to a simmer and keep hot.

Heat a wide frying pan over high heat. When pan is hot, add 2 tablespoons of the oil. When oil is hot, add mushrooms and stir-fry for 1 minute. Add sherry and sugar and stir-fry until liquid evaporates; remove mushrooms and set aside. Reduce heat to medium and add the remaining 2 tablespoons oil. Cook bean curd until flecked with brown (about 3 minutes on each side). Return mushrooms to pan. Stir cooking sauce, pour into pan, and cook, stirring gently, until sauce bubbles and thickens. Keep hot.

Bring seasoned water to a boil. Drop in vegetables. Cook until crisp-tender (about 4 minutes); drain, then discard ginger. To serve, arrange vegetables around edges of a serving platter. Pour bean curd mixture into center. Makes 4 or 5 servings.

Cooking sauce. In a bowl, blend ½ cup **chicken broth** or water, 2 tablespoons **oyster sauce**, 1 tablespoon **dry sherry**, 1 teaspoon **sugar**, 2 teaspoons **cornstarch**, and ¼ teaspoon **sesame oil.**

Bean Curd Szechwan-style

You need a bowl of plain steamed rice to temper the red-hot spiciness of this succulent dish. To make an easy meal of it, prepare the bean curd dish first, since it can take reheating—then stir-fry a vegetable for a crisp, soothing contrast.

- ½ to ⅔ pound bean curd or tofu
- 1 teaspoon *each* soy sauce and dry sherry
- 1 teaspoon sweet bean sauce or hoi-sin sauce
- ¼ pound boneless lean pork, finely chopped or ground
- 3 tablespoons salad oil
- 1 teaspoon minced fresh ginger
- 2 teaspoons minced garlic
- 2 teaspoons hot bean sauce or 2 small, dry, hot chile peppers, crumbled and seeded, if desired
- ¾ cup water
- 2 tablespoons soy sauce
- 2 whole green onions, thinly sliced
- 2 tablespoons *each* cornstarch and water
- ½ teaspoon roasted and crushed Szechwan peppercorns, page 13 (optional)

Cut bean curd in ½-inch cubes; place in a colander and let drain for 15 minutes. In a bowl, blend the 1 teaspoon soy, sherry, and sweet bean sauce; add meat and stir to coat. Stir in 1 teaspoon of the oil; let stand for 15 minutes to marinate.

Heat a wok or wide frying pan over high heat. When pan is hot, add remaining oil. When oil begins to heat, add ginger and garlic. Stir once, then add meat and stir-fry until meat is no longer pink (about 2 minutes). Stir in hot bean sauce. Add drained bean curd, water, and the 2 tablespoons soy. Simmer for 3 minutes, then add green onion. Blend cornstarch and water, add to pan, and cook, stirring, until sauce bubbles and thickens. Sprinkle with crushed peppercorns just before serving. Makes 2 or 3 servings.

Chicken Custard Soup

Unlike most Chinese dishes which are meant for sharing, this delicate soup should be prepared in indi-vidual bowls so the smooth soup, velvety custard, and succulent meat come together in each spoonful. It makes an elegant first course for a Chinese meal, or serve it as a delicious light lunch.

- 4 medium-size dried mushrooms
- 3½ cups chicken broth, page 24 or canned
- 2 eggs
- ⅛ teaspoon ground ginger
  Dash of white pepper
- 1 teaspoon soy sauce
- ¾ pound chicken breasts, skinned, boned, and cut in ¼-inch-wide strips
- ½ pound spinach (stems removed), cut in ¼-inch-wide strips
- 2 tablespoons cornstarch
- 3 tablespoons water

Cover mushrooms with warm water, let stand for 30 minutes, then drain. Cut off and discard stems; squeeze mushrooms dry and thinly slice. In a pan, heat 1½ cups of the chicken broth to simmering. Add mushrooms and simmer for 5 minutes. Remove mushrooms with a slotted spoon and distribute among 4 heatproof bowls (each about 1½ to 2 cups capacity). In another bowl, beat eggs. Gradually stir hot broth into eggs. Pour equal amount of egg mixture over mushrooms in the 4 bowls.

Set bowls in a deep baking pan and place baking pan in a 350° oven; pour boiling water into pan as high as level of custard in the bowls. Bake for about 18 to 20 minutes or until a knife inserted in custard comes out clean. Remove from oven; remove bowls from water and set aside. (Custard may cool slightly, but will be reheated when you pour the hot soup over it.)

Place remaining 2 cups broth in a pan. Season with ginger, pepper, and soy. When custard is done, heat broth to boiling and add chicken. Cook, stirring, until chicken loses its pinkness (about 3 minutes). Add spinach. Blend cornstarch and water, add to soup, and cook, stirring, until slightly thickened (about 1 minute). To serve, ladle hot soup over custard in each bowl. Makes 4 servings.

Silver Thread Stirred Eggs

Slippery bean threads give a bouncy lightness to scrambled eggs laced with meat and vegeta-bles. For an easy meal, serve this with rice and a small side dish of cold spiced cabbage (page 79).

- 2 ounces dried bean threads
- 4 medium-size dried mushrooms
- 2 teaspoons soy sauce
- 6 eggs
- ½ teaspoon salt
- ⅛ teaspoon white pepper
- 2 tablespoons salad oil
- 1 clove garlic, minced
- 4 ounces cooked ham, cut in match-stick pieces
- 1 stalk celery, thinly sliced crosswise
- ¼ cup sliced bamboo shoots
- 2 whole green onions, thinly sliced

Cover bean threads with warm water and let stand for 30 minutes. Drain, then place on a cutting board and cut in 4-inch lengths. Cover mushrooms with ¾ cup warm water and let stand for 30 minutes. Remove mushrooms from water, then pour off ½ cup of water into a bowl and discard sandy water that remains. Add soy to mushroom water. Cut off and discard mushroom stems; squeeze mushrooms dry and slice thinly. In a bowl, beat eggs with salt and pepper.

Heat a wok or wide frying pan over high heat. When pan is hot, add oil. When oil begins to heat, add garlic. Stir once, then add ham and mushrooms and stir-fry for 1 minute. Add celery and bamboo shoots and stir-fry for 2 minutes. Add bean threads and mushroom water and cook until liquid is ab-sorbed. Add green onion and cook for 30 seconds. Reduce heat to medium. Pour eggs into pan. Turning occasionally with a wide spatula, cook eggs until they are soft and creamy. Makes 4 servings.

For brunch, lunch, or a quick snack, try Hot & Sour Eggs in a Noodle Nest (recipe on page 68). Vary the vegeta-ble in the sauce to fit the season.

Hot & Sour Eggs in a Noodle Nest

(Pictured on page 67)

For an unusual brunch or luncheon dish, slide hot poached eggs into a nest of tender noodles and top with a mildly seasoned vegetable sauce. If you wish, the eggs can be cooked in advance, drained, and chilled. Before serving, drop them in a pan of hot (not boiling) water for 5 minutes to heat through.

- 1 **cup chicken broth, page 24 or canned**
- 2 **tablespoons** *each* **cornstarch and white vinegar**
- 1 **teaspoon** *each* **soy sauce and sugar**
- ⅛ **teaspoon white pepper**
- ½ **pound Chinese noodles (page 81) or fine spaghetti, cooked, drained, and hot**
- 1 **teaspoon sesame oil**
- 1 **tablespoon soy sauce**
- 1 **tablespoon salad oil**
- 2 **cups bok choy, cut in 2-inch lengths, or ½ pound asparagus (tough ends removed), cut in 2-inch slanting slices**
- 1 **tablespoon water**
- 1 **whole green onion, thinly sliced**
- 4 **hot poached eggs**

In a bowl, blend chicken broth, cornstarch, vinegar, the 1 teaspoon soy, sugar, and white pepper; set aside. Toss hot noodles with the sesame oil and the 1 tablespoon soy.

Heat a wok or wide frying pan over high heat. When pan is hot, add the 1 tablespoon oil. When oil is hot, add bok choy or asparagus. Stir-fry for 1 minute. Add water, cover, and cook until vegetable is crisp-tender (about 2 minutes for bok choy, 3 minutes for asparagus). Add green onion and cook for 30 seconds. Stir chicken broth mixture, add to pan, and cook, stirring, until sauce bubbles and thickens.

To serve, arrange noodles into nest shapes on 4 serving plates. Slide a hot poached egg into each nest, then spoon over vegetable sauce. Makes 4 servings.

Marbled Tea Eggs

(Pictured on page 83)

Usually these eggs are cut in quarters and served as part of a cold appetizer selection. But they are so pretty—with a marbling of fine dark lines—that, if you serve them for hors d'oeuvres, you may want to present the whole shelled eggs nestled in shredded lettuce and slice them to order. They make a fine addition to picnic fare, too.

- 8 **eggs**
- 3 **black-tea bags or 3 teaspoons loose black tea**
- 2 **tablespoons soy sauce**
- 1 **tablespoon salt**
- 1 **whole star anise (or 1 teaspoon anise seeds and a 2-inch stick of cinnamon)**

Place eggs in a pan and cover with cold water. Bring water to simmering and cook for 20 minutes. Drain; rinse eggs with cold water until cool enough to handle. Gently crack shells of eggs with back of a spoon until there is a fine network of cracks, but do not remove shells.

Return eggs to pan. Add 4 cups water, the tea, soy, salt, and star anise. Heat to simmering and cook, on low heat, for 1 hour. Cool and chill eggs in the liquid for at least 8 hours or up to 2 days. Shell eggs before serving. Makes 8 eggs.

Shrimp Egg Foo Yung

Canton

You can make these colorful patties with shrimp or crab. The vegetables inside are crunchy, the egg soft and creamy.

- ¼ **pound green beans**
  About ¼ cup salad oil
- 1 **clove garlic, minced**
- ¼ **pound medium-size raw shrimp, shelled, deveined, and coarsely chopped, or ⅓ pound flaked crab meat**
  Foo yung sauce (directions follow)
- 1 **carrot, shredded**
- 6 **eggs**
- 1 **teaspoon salt**
- ¼ **teaspoon white pepper**

Remove ends and strings from green beans. Cut crosswise in ⅛-inch-thick diagonal slices. (To make cutting faster, place 4 or 5 beans in an even row on cutting board and cut through all at the same time.)

Heat a wide frying pan over high heat. When pan is hot, add 2 tablespoons of the oil. When oil begins to heat, add garlic. Stir once, then add shrimp and stir-fry for 1 minute. (If you use crab, do not add until after the vegetables are cooked.) Add beans and carrot, reduce heat to medium, and stir-fry until vegetables are crisp-tender (about 2 minutes). Remove from pan and cool.

Prepare foo yung sauce. Beat eggs with salt and pepper, then stir in cooled shrimp-vegetable mixture.

Heat 2 more tablespoons oil in

pan over medium-high heat. When oil is hot, measure ¼ cup of egg mixture for each patty, cook like pancakes, and make 3 or 4 at a time. When egg is set, turn to cook other side. Fry until golden. Remove to a heated serving platter and keep warm. Repeat until all patties have been cooked, adding more oil as needed. Pour hot foo yung sauce over patties and serve at once. Makes 6 servings.

Foo yung sauce. In a pan, heat 1 cup **chicken broth,** 1 tablespoon **soy sauce,** and 2 teaspoons *each* **sugar** and **vinegar.** Blend 1 tablespoon **cornstarch** with 2 tablespoons **water.** Add to sauce and cook, stirring, until sauce bubbles and thickens.

Egg Crescents
Shanghai

These little egg patties are very hard to stop eating. Serve them unadorned for appetizers, or with Chinese cabbage as a main dish.

2 medium-size dried mushrooms
¼ pound boneless lean pork, finely chopped or ground
½ teaspoon sugar
1 teaspoon soy sauce
1½ teaspoons dry sherry
¼ teaspoon *each* salt and minced fresh ginger
4 eggs
¼ teaspoon salt
About 3 tablespoons salad oil
Stir-fried Chinese cabbage (directions follow)

Cover mushrooms with warm water, let stand for 30 minutes, then drain. Cut off and discard stems; squeeze mushrooms dry and finely chop. Mix together mushrooms, pork, sugar, soy, sherry, the ¼ teaspoon salt, and ginger. Beat eggs with the other ¼ teaspoon salt.

Heat a wide frying pan over medium heat.

When pan is hot, add 2 tablespoons of the oil. When oil is hot, ladle 2 tablespoons of beaten egg into pan in a circular motion so it forms a 3-inch circle. Place 2 teaspoons pork filling in center of egg.

When egg sets on the bottom but is still liquid on top, fold circle in half with a spatula and turn over; press crescent together gently to seal. Push to side of pan and make a second circle. Continue cooking and turning first crescent for about 4 minutes or until filling is no longer pink (cut to test). Remove to a warm platter and keep hot. Repeat, adding more oil as needed, until all crescents have been cooked. Serve as appetizers or arrange on a bed of stir-fried Chinese cabbage and serve as a main dish. Makes 4 servings.

Stir-fried Chinese cabbage. Cut enough **Chinese cabbage leaves** (napa cabbage) into 1 by 2-inch pieces to make 2 cups. Heat a wok or wide frying pan over high heat. When pan is hot, add 1 tablespoon **salad oil.** When oil is hot, add cabbage and stir-fry until crisp-tender (about 3 minutes). Add a few drops **water** if cabbage begins to stick but be certain all liquid has evaporated from pan before serving. Season to taste with **salt** and **white pepper.**

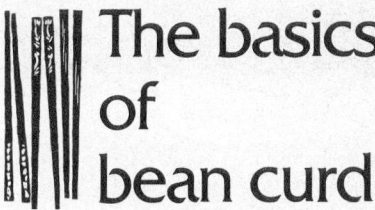

The basics of bean curd

We Occidentals are becoming savvy. In recent years we've learned what Oriental cooks have known for centuries—that a wide range of superb dishes and an important source of inexpensive, low-fat protein stem from a derivative of soybeans. The Japanese call it tofu. The Chinese call it bean curd.

If you have never eaten bean curd, your first taste may be a disappointment. The texture is silky and smooth, the color creamy white, but the flavor is bland and neutral. What we may dismiss as tastelessness, however, is actually bean curd's basic asset, for it readily absorbs the flavors of other foods and sauces. Stir-fried with chili peppers it is hot and spicy; simmered with oyster sauce it is rich and mellow;

dressed with sugar, vinegar, and sesame oil it is light and sweet.

Once confined to Oriental food stores, bean curd is becoming increasingly available at supermarkets and natural food stores. It comes in many forms—fresh, dried, fermented, and fried; but throughout this book we explore ways to use the fresh Chinese bean curd (sometimes labeled soybean cake) and Japanese tofu. Bean curd, which has a lower water content than tofu, is firmer and better suited to withstand the rigors of stir-frying, but you can prepare these recipes with tofu, too.

Look for bean curd in the produce section of your market. It is sold water-packed in plastic containers. There are usually 4 slices in a container, each slice weighing about 6 ounces. (Tofu is usually sold in a solid block weighing about 1 pound.)

Store bean curd in the refrigerator. Before using, drain and rinse with cold water. To store any leftover bean curd, place it in a plastic container, cover with fresh water, seal, and refrigerate up to a week.

Vegetables

Basic Stir-fried Vegetables

Probably no other technique of Chinese cooking is as well known as stir-frying, and no ingredient as well suited for stir-frying as vegetables. With their crisp textures, bright colors, and sweet natural flavors, vegetables tumble to perfection when fast cooked in a wok. Served plain or with a light gravy, they enhance any meal.

The stir-fry technique is fascinating to watch. What appears at first to be complicated is deceptively simple to do if you understand the basic rules. On page 10, we explain and show you how to stir-fry a dish that contains vegetables with meat, poultry, or seafood. To cook vegetables alone, you follow the same technique.

Season your wok. Place a wok or wide frying pan over high heat. When the pan is hot, add a small amount of oil and heat until the oil ripples slightly but is not smoking. Lift the pan and swirl the oil around the bottom and sides. At this point you add your seasonings, such as ginger and garlic, and cook just until fragrant. Chinese cooks call this step "seasoning the wok," and it takes only a few seconds—any longer and the seasonings burn. If your oil begins to smoke, lift the pan off the heat for a moment to cool the oil.

Add vegetables to the seasoned wok and stir-fry until all are coated with oil. What you do next depends on the vegetable. With a few, you continue stir-frying to complete the cooking, but most need a little more liquid to become tender. Add the liquid by pouring it around the sides of your pan, then cover and cook until vegetables are crisp and tender. (One of the advantages of using a

Heart-warming Fish-stuffed Bean Curd (recipe on page 64) cooks and comes to the table in Chinese clay pot. Sprout & Cress Salad (recipe on page 77) and mandarin oranges complete the meal.

Freshness is the most important quality a Chinese cook looks for in vegetables. As one Hong Kong food expert expressed it, "We would rather cook a vegetable that was unusual, if it was fresh, than settle for the tried and true, if it looked limp and tired."

Because the land of China spans such diverse growing conditions, the country produces a tremendous variety of vegetables. If you visit Oriental markets in America you will find a multitude of leaf and root vegetables that may not look familiar to you but are well known to Chinese cooks. If you enjoy gardening, buy Oriental vegetable seeds and you can grow wondrous squashes, greens, and gourds, all exciting to discover.

In this chapter, though, we talk about ways to prepare superb vegetable dishes with only a visit to your neighborhood market. We outline the basics of the stir-fry technique which you can use to cook almost any vegetable. Then we offer vegetable dishes that are favorites in Chinese home-style and restaurant cooking.

wok is that the hot sides immediately heat the liquid and ensure uninterrupted cooking.) It is better to add too little rather than too much liquid. If the pan becomes dry before the vegetables are done, you can lift the lid and add a few more drops.

Following the basic recipe, we list cutting suggestions, amounts of liquid to add, and cooking times for each vegetable. Use them as flexible guidelines because the way you cut a vegetable, its freshness, the size of your wok or pan, and the intensity of the heat you use all affect the cooking time.

Stir-frying is very active cooking. The variables demand your immediate attention; but after you stir-fry a vegetable once or twice in your own wok on your own range, it will become a natural skill.

> **Optional cooking sauce:** ½ **cup chicken broth or water, 1 tablespoon cornstarch, and 2 teaspoons soy sauce**
> 2 tablespoons salad oil
> ½ teaspoon minced fresh ginger
> 1 small clove garlic, minced
> 1 pound cut vegetables (directions follow for individual vegetables)
> ½ teaspoon *each* salt and sugar
> Chicken broth or water

If you wish to serve a vegetable with a sauce, combine chicken broth, cornstarch, and soy, and set

aside. Heat a wok or wide frying pan over high heat. When pan is hot, add oil. When oil begins to heat, add ginger and garlic. Stir once around pan. Add vegetables and stir-fry for 1 minute to coat with oil. Add salt, sugar, and liquid; cover and cook until vegetables are crisp-tender.

If you wish to cook several vegetables and the textures are different, add the firmest vegetable to the pan first and partially cook; then add the more tender vegetables near the end of the cooking time. Or better yet, you can cook each vegetable separately and combine them for reheating and blending of flavors.

Serve at once, or stir cooking sauce, add to pan, and cook, stirring, until sauce bubbles and thickens (about 30 seconds). Makes 4 servings.

Asparagus. Cut in ¼-inch slanting slices. Stir-fry for 1 minute. Add 2 tablespoons liquid, cover, and cook for 2 to 3 minutes.

Bean sprouts. Leave whole. Stir-fry for 1 minute. Add a few drops liquid and toss for 1 to 2 minutes.

Bok choy. Cut stems in ½-inch slanting slices; cut leaves in 2-inch pieces. Stir-fry stems for 1 minute. Add leaves and stir-fry for 30 seconds. Add 1 tablespoon liquid, cover, and cook for 2 to 3 minutes.

Broccoli. Cut off flowerets and slash their stems. Peel thick stalks, then thinly slice or cut in matchstick pieces. Stir-fry for 1 minute. Add 2 tablespoons liquid, cover, and cook for 3 to 4 minutes.

Brussels sprouts. Cut in half. Stir-fry for 1 minute. Add 4 tablespoons liquid, cover, and cook for 5 minutes.

Cabbage (all varieties). Cut in ¼-inch slices or 1-inch pieces. Stir-fry for 1 minute. Add 1 tablespoon liquid, cover, and cook for 2 minutes.

Carrot. Cut in ¼-inch slanting slices. Stir-fry for 1 minute. Add 3 tablespoons liquid, cover, and cook for 3 to 4 minutes.

Cauliflower. Cut in small flowerets, then in ½-inch pieces. Stir-fry for 1 minute. Add 3 tablespoons liquid, cover, and cook for 3 to 4 minutes.

Celery. Cut in ¼-inch slanting slices. Stir-fry for 1 minute. Add a few drops liquid and toss for 1 minute.

Eggplant. Peel, then cut in cubes or finger-size pieces. Stir-fry for 1 minute. Add 4 tablespoons liquid, cover, and cook for 5 to 6 minutes.

Green beans. Cut in 1-inch lengths. Stir-fry for 1 minute. Add 3 tablespoons liquid, cover, and cook for 4 minutes.

Lettuce. Cut in 2-inch squares or ½-inch strips. Stir-fry for 1 minute.

Mushrooms (fresh). Slice through stems in ¼-inch slices. Stir-fry for 1 minute. Add 1 tablespoon liquid and toss for 2 minutes.

Onions. Cut in wedges or slice. Stir-fry for 1 to 2 minutes.

Peppers (red and green bell). Seed, cut in 1-inch pieces or ¼-inch slices. Stir-fry for 1 minute. Add 1 tablespoon liquid and toss for 1 minute.

Snow peas. Break off ends and remove strings. Stir-fry for 1 minute.

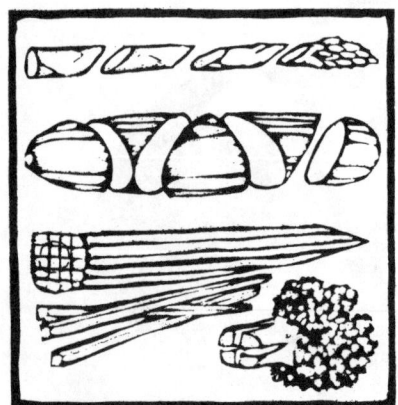

Cut asparagus (top) in slanting slices. Roll-cut zucchini: slice down, turn a quarter-turn, slice again. Slice carrot lengthwise, then cut each slice again into matchstick pieces. Slash broccoli for fast cooking.

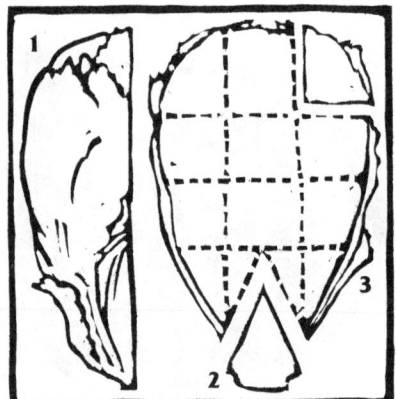

The natural shape of a vegetable determines the cutting style. Split Chinese cabbage (napa cabbage) in half lengthwise; remove V-shaped core. Cut leaves in sections and separate layers for stir-frying.

Add 1 tablespoon liquid and toss for 1 minute.

Spinach. Cut in 2-inch-wide strips. Stir-fry for 1 minute. Add a few drops liquid, cover, and cook for 1 minute.

Swiss chard. Cut in 1-inch slices. Stir-fry for 1 minute. Add 1 tablespoon liquid, cover, and cook for 2 minutes.

Tomatoes. Cut in wedges. Stir-fry for 1 to 2 minutes.

Zucchini (and all summer squash varieties). Cut in ¼-inch slanting slices or wedges. Stir-fry for 1 minute. Add 1 tablespoon liquid, cover, and cook for 3 minutes.

Eggplant Szechwan-style

This recipe is an example of how Chinese cooks stretch a small amount of meat and, at the same time, give vegetables a rich meaty flavor. If your wok is carbon steel, use a frying pan (not cast iron) to prepare this dish. The metal does not affect the flavor, but causes the eggplant to turn overly dark.

½ cup chicken broth, page 24 or canned
1 teaspoon *each* sugar and vinegar
1 tablespoon soy sauce
½ teaspoon salt
   Dash of pepper
1 large eggplant or 1¼ pounds Oriental eggplant
5 tablespoons salad oil
¼ pound boneless lean pork, finely chopped or ground
2 whole green onions, finely chopped
1 teaspoon minced fresh ginger
2 teaspoons minced garlic
2 teaspoons hot bean sauce or 2 small, dry, hot chile peppers, crumbled and seeded, if desired
1 teaspoon cornstarch
1 tablespoon water
1 teaspoon sesame oil

In a bowl combine chicken broth, sugar, vinegar, soy, salt, and pepper; set aside. Peel eggplant and cut in strips 2 inches long and ½ inch thick. (Do not peel if you use Oriental eggplant.)

Heat a wok or wide frying pan over medium-high heat. When pan is hot, add 3 tablespoons of the oil. When oil is hot, add eggplant and stir-fry for 3 minutes. (Eggplant will soak up the oil immediately; stir continuously to prevent burning.) Remove from pan. Heat the remaining 2 tablespoons oil in pan. Add pork, onion, ginger, garlic, and hot bean sauce. Stir-fry until meat is no longer pink (about 2 minutes). Return eggplant to pan, pour in chicken broth mixture, cover, and cook over medium-low heat until eggplant is tender (about 6 minutes). Blend cornstarch and water, pour into pan and cook, stirring, until sauce bubbles and thickens. Stir in sesame oil just before serving. Makes 4 servings.

Dry-fried Beans
Szechwan

Chinese cooking often combines several techniques to create unusual flavors and textures. In this dish you first deep-fry green beans to give them a chewy texture. Then, when you stir-try them, they absorb all the seasoning but still remain crisp. The result is a full-flavored dish with very little sauce.

1 tablespoon *each* soy sauce and dry sherry
2 tablespoons chicken broth or water
1 teaspoon sugar
1 tablespoon dried shrimp
1 small piece Szechwan preserved turnip
1 pound green beans
   Salad oil
¼ pound boneless lean pork, finely chopped or ground
1 whole green onion, thinly sliced
2 teaspoons sesame oil

In a bowl, combine soy, sherry, chicken broth, and sugar; set aside. Cover dried shrimp with hot water, let stand for 30 minutes, then drain. Finely chop shrimp. Rinse turnip to eliminate red pickling spice, and finely chop; you should have 1 tablespoon. Wash beans and pat dry. Cut off ends and remove strings. Cut beans in 3-inch lengths.

In a wok or wide frying pan, pour salad oil to a depth of 1 inch and heat to 375° on a deep-frying thermometer. Add beans, a handful at a time, and cook, stirring occasionally, until beans are wrinkled and blistered (about 3 minutes). Remove each batch with a slotted spoon and drain on paper towels. At this point you can cool, cover, and refrigerate beans until next day.

Pour off all but 2 tablespoons of the oil and heat pan over high heat. When oil is hot, add pork and stir-fry until meat is no longer pink (about 2 minutes). Add chopped shrimp and turnip. Stir-fry for 1 minute. Return beans to pan along with onion. Pour in soy mixture and stir and cook until beans absorb the sauce. Stir in sesame oil just before serving. Makes 4 servings.

Cold-stirred Lima Beans

Peking   (Pictured on page 18)

The sweet nutlike flavor of lima beans and the crunchy texture of bamboo shoots makes this a refreshing dish to serve with spicy Chinese food or as part of an appetizer cold plate.

  2 **tablespoons salad oil**
  1 **package (10 oz.) frozen baby lima beans, thawed**
  ½ **cup diced bamboo shoots**
  ½ **cup chicken broth, page 24 or canned**
  2 **teaspoons sugar**
  ¾ **teaspoon salt**
  ½ **teaspoon sesame oil**

Heat a wok or wide frying pan over high heat. When pan is hot, add oil. When oil is hot, add lima beans and bamboo shoots. Stir-fry for 1 minute. Add chicken broth, sugar, and salt. Cover and simmer, stirring occasionally, until beans are crisp-tender (about 5 minutes). Remove cover and continue cooking until all liquid evaporates. Stir in sesame oil. Cool, cover, and chill. Serve cold. Makes 6 servings.

Creamed Chinese Cabbage

Shanghai

Milk is seldom used in Chinese cooking, but in this traditional recipe it is combined with chicken fat to bring out the delicate sweetness of cabbage. Unlike most crisp-

textured, stir-fried vegetables, this cabbage should be meltingly tender.

  ½ **cup chicken broth, page 24 or canned**
  1 **teaspoon salt**
  ½ **teaspoon sugar**
  1½ **pounds Chinese cabbage (napa cabbage)**
  1 **tablespoon rendered chicken fat or salad oil**
  ¼ **cup milk**
  2 **tablespoons cornstarch**
  ¼ **cup finely chopped ham**

In a bowl, combine chicken broth, salt, and sugar. Split cabbage lengthwise and core. Cut leaves and stems in 2-inch pieces. Heat a wok or wide frying pan over high heat. When pan is hot, add chicken fat. When fat is hot, add cabbage and stir-fry for 30 seconds. Pour in broth mixture and cover pan. Reduce heat to medium and cook until cabbage is tender (about 5 minutes). Remove cabbage with a slotted spoon, drain briefly, and place on a hot serving platter. Blend milk and cornstarch. Increase heat to high, add cornstarch mixture to pan and cook, stirring, until sauce bubbles and thickens. Pour sauce over cabbage and garnish with ham. Makes 4 servings.

Bean Sprouts & Carrot

Bean sprouts have a high water content, so in order to keep them crisp you need to stir-fry them quickly over very high heat. If you double this recipe, cook it in two batches.

  1 **tablespoon white vinegar**
  2 **teaspoons sugar**
  ½ **teaspoon salt**
  1 **teaspoon soy sauce**
  1 **pound bean sprouts**
  1 **tablespoon salad oil**
  1 **carrot, shredded**
  1 **whole green onion, thinly sliced**

In a bowl, combine vinegar, sugar, salt, and soy. Wash bean sprouts

and drain well. (For banquet-style cooking, Chinese chefs remove the tail ends from the bean sprouts.) Heat a wok or wide frying pan over high heat. When pan is hot, add oil. When oil is hot, add sprouts, carrot, and onion, and stir-fry for 1 minute. Pour in vinegar mixture and continue stir-frying until bean sprouts are crisp-tender (about 2 minutes). Makes 4 servings.

Shrimp-stuffed Mushrooms

Shanghai   (Pictured on opposite page)

The versatile shrimp filling used to make shrimp balls or shrimp toast can also be used to stuff mushrooms. Rich flavored dried mushrooms definitely make more flavorful containers for the light filling, but if you cannot find even, well shaped ones, substitute fresh mushrooms. Serve them as a hot appetizer, first course, or as part of a Chinese meal.

  16 **medium-size dried mushrooms or 2-inch-diameter fresh mushrooms**
  ½ **teaspoon *each* salt and sugar**
  1 **tablespoon soy sauce**
  1 **cup chicken broth, page 24 or canned**
      Shrimp filling (page 22)
  1½ **teaspoons cornstarch**
  1 **tablespoon water**

Cover dried mushrooms with warm water, let stand for 30 minutes, then drain. Cut off and discard stems. Place mushrooms in a pan with salt, sugar, soy, and chicken broth. Bring to a boil, then reduce heat, cover, and simmer for 30 minutes. If you use fresh mushrooms, simmer in chicken broth mixture for only 10 minutes. Remove mushrooms

---

Dried mushrooms make flavorful containers for a savory shrimp stuffing (recipe on this page). Complement these appetizers with a light, fruity white wine.

from broth (reserve broth), drain, and cool slightly.

Mound approximately 2 teaspoons shrimp filling in each mushroom. Arrange mushrooms, filled side up, on one or two serving plates that will fit inside a steamer. At this point you can cover and refrigerate for as long as 8 hours, but bring to room temperature before steaming.

To cook, place plate on rack in steamer, cover, and steam over boiling water for 10 minutes. If you cook this on two plates, serve the first portion while you cook the second. In a pan, heat ½ cup of the reserved broth. Blend cornstarch and water. Add to pan, and cook, stirring, until sauce bubbles and thickens. Pour sauce over hot mushrooms just before serving. Makes 16.

Vegetable Pickles
Canton   (Pictured on page 18)

Even when pickled, vegetables are cut in bite-size pieces so they can easily be picked up with chopsticks. You can pickle a single vegetable or a mixture to serve as crisp appetizers or small chow (side dish) at any meal.

- 1 **pound assorted vegetables such as carrots, celery, green beans, red bell or green pepper, Chinese cabbage (napa cabbage), and bok choy**
- 2 **tablespoons salt**
- 1 **cup water**
- ½ **cup white vinegar**
- 3 **tablespoons sugar**
- 1 **small, dry, hot chile pepper, crumbled and seeded, if desired, or 1 teaspoon crushed red pepper**

Wash and prepare vegetables. Peel carrots and cut in ¼-inch-thick slanting slices. Cut celery in ¾-inch-wide slanting slices. Cut off ends and remove strings from green beans; cut in 2-inch lengths. Seed red and green pepper and cut in 1-inch squares. Core cabbage and cut leaves in 1-inch squares. Remove bok choy leaves (reserve for other use) and cut stems in 1-inch lengths. Place prepared vegetables in a bowl, sprinkle with salt, and stir until well mixed. Cover and chill overnight.

The next day, heat water, vinegar, sugar, and chile until sugar is dissolved; let cool. Pour liquid off salted vegetables, but do not wash with water. Pack vegetables into a 1 pint jar. Cover with cooled pickling liquid (brine). If vegetables are

How to make a phoenix nest

(Yam nest pictured on page 78)

A basket of golden potato shreds, called a phoenix nest, makes a handsome showcase for almost any stir-fried dish. In Chinese restaurants, one large nest holds an entrée for several people. After you eat the contents, you break the nest apart with fingers and nibble. At home, you can make one large nest or several small ones for individual servings.

The cooking is simple and can be done a day in advance. Plan your equipment first. You need two sieves of the same size, one to act as a form that gives shape to the shredded potato, and one to hold the shreds in place as they cook. To hold the cooking oil, use a deep pan, about 6 inches in diameter, in which the sieves will fit comfortably; or use a wok. To determine how much oil to use, place an empty sieve in the pan, then pour in enough oil to cover at least three-fourths of the sieve.

By following the same cooking technique, you can make a nest out of potato, sweet potato, yam, or taro root. If made ahead, stack nests, separated by paper towels, and seal in a plastic bag. Store at room temperature for up to 2 days. Because the nests are an open mesh rather than a solid layer, plan to fill them with a stir-fried dish that has a light glaze rather than a heavy gravy.

Potato nest. Peel 2 medium-size **white new potatoes** and shred them lengthwise to make long strips; you should have 2 cups. Squeeze potato, by the handful, to eliminate liquid, then place in a bowl. Sprinkle 1 tablespoon **cornstarch** over potato and toss to distribute cornstarch evenly and loosen shreds. Arrange a handful of shreds inside one sieve in a latticework over the bottom and at least halfway up the side. Fit second sieve inside first one. Heat **oil** to 325° on a deep-frying thermometer, place sieve in pan, and cook nest until golden brown (about 3 or 4 minutes). Remove from oil and lift off top sieve. Loosen edges of nest with tip of a sharp knife, then gently remove nest and drain on paper towels. Makes 4 or 5 4-inch nests.

Yam or sweet potato nest. Follow directions for potato nest, but substitute 2 cups shredded sweet potatoes or yams for potatoes, and increase temperature of cooking oil to 350°. Cook yam nests until a light pumpkin color (about 4 to 5 minutes). Cook sweet potato nests until golden brown (about 3 to 4 minutes).

Taro nest. Follow directions for potato nest, but substitute 2 cups shredded taro root for potatoes; do not squeeze liquid from shredded taro; and eliminate the cornstarch. Heat oil to 350° on a deep-frying thermometer. Cook taro nests until golden brown (about 3 to 4 minutes).

not completely submerged, push crumpled plastic wrap in jar to bring brine level to the top. Cover and refrigerate for 2 days before serving. To serve, remove vegetables with a slotted spoon and serve in a small bowl. You can keep extra vegetables refrigerated in the brine up to a week. Makes 1 pint.

Marinated Lotus Root
(Pictured on page 23)

It is worthwhile to look in Oriental markets for fresh lotus root. No other vegetable can quite match its sweet flavor, crunchy texture, and naturally beautiful cut-out design. But we also tell you how to prepare familiar vegetables, such as carrots and snow peas, this same way to serve as crisp appetizers.

- 1 pound fresh lotus root
- 1 tablespoon *each* soy sauce and white vinegar
- 2 teaspoons sugar
- ¼ teaspoon salt
- 1 teaspoon sesame oil

Peel lotus root, discard both ends, and cut in ⅛-inch-thick slices. Place in cold water to prevent discoloring, but drain before cooking. Bring a pan of water to boiling. Add lotus root and cook for 3 minutes. Lotus root should be crisp-tender. Drain, rinse with cold water, and drain again.

In a plastic bag, mix the soy, vinegar, sugar, salt, and sesame oil. Place drained lotus root in the bag and seal. Refrigerate, turning bag occasionally to distribute marinade, for at least 1 hour or as long as 8 hours. To serve, arrange lotus root on a serving plate and pour over any remaining marinade. Makes 8 servings.

注意 **Marinated carrots.** Cut 1 pound carrots in ⅛-inch slices. Follow directions for lotus root, but cook for 4 minutes.

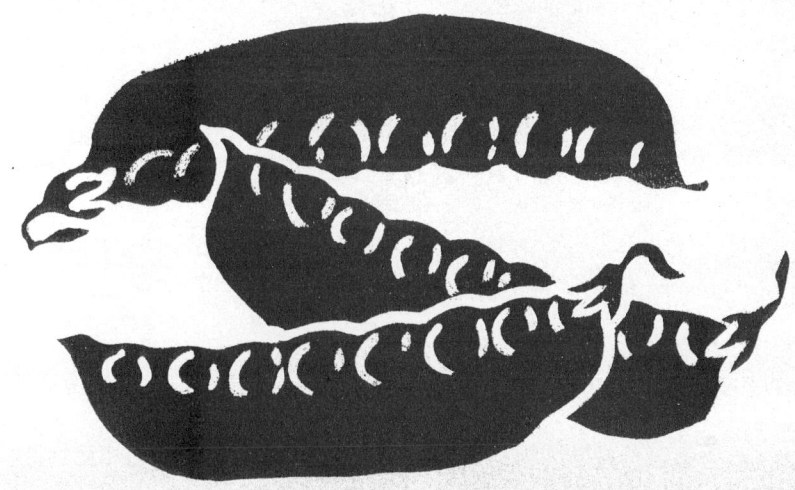

注意 **Marinated snow peas.** Cut off ends and remove strings from ½ pound snow peas. Follow directions for cooking lotus root, but cook for 1½ minutes.

Sesame Eggplant Salad
(Pictured on page 18)

Chinese-style cold vegetable tidbits are ideal to include in a company menu. The cooking can be done in advance and the last minute assembly is minimal.

- 1 large eggplant or 1¼ pounds Oriental eggplant
- 1½ tablespoons *each* sesame seeds and salad oil
- 1 teaspoon *each* minced garlic and fresh ginger
- 1 tablespoon *each* soy sauce and vinegar
- ½ teaspoon sugar
- 2 whole green onions

Pierce eggplant in several places. Bake, uncovered, in a 400° oven until very soft (about 1 hour for regular eggplant, 45 minutes for Oriental eggplant). Cool; pull off and discard skin. Tear flesh into shreds and discard any big seed pockets. Cover and chill for as long as 2 days.

In a small frying pan, cook sesame seeds in oil over low heat until golden (about 2 minutes). Stir in garlic and ginger, then remove pan from heat. Let cool. Stir in soy, vinegar, and sugar. Cover and chill.

Before serving, place eggplant in a colander and drain very well. Thinly slice green onion and stir into eggplant along with sesame dressing. Makes 4 servings.

Sprout & Cress Salad
(Pictured on page 70)

The Chinese serve few salads such as we know them. This exception, made with crisp bean sprouts and spicy watercress, as well as the variation made with cucumber, would be at home in either a Chinese or Western meal.

- ¾ pound bean sprouts
- 1 bunch watercress
- 2 tablespoons soy sauce
- 1 tablespoon *each* vinegar and sesame oil
- 1 teaspoon sugar

Heat a large pan of water to boiling. Drop in bean sprouts and cook for 30 seconds. Drain, rinse with cold water, and drain again;

chill. Break watercress into 2-inch lengths and discard any tough stems. Stir together soy, vinegar, sesame oil, and sugar. Just before serving, drain bean sprouts again, then combine with watercress and dressing. Toss until vegetables are well coated. Makes 4 servings.

注意 **Sprout and cucumber salad.** Follow the directions for sprout salad, but substitute 1 cup **shredded peeled cucumber** for the watercress.

Sweet & Sour Carrots

This not too sweet sauce intensifies the natural sweetness of carrots. For variety, you can prepare cauliflower or green beans the same way.

- ¼ **cup chicken broth, page 24 or canned**
- 2 **tablespoons** *each* **vinegar and brown sugar**
- 1 **teaspoon salt**
- 1 **tablespoon cornstarch**
- 1 **tablespoon salad oil**
- 1 **pound carrots, cut in ¼-inch-thick slanting slices**
- 1 **small onion, cut in half, then crosswise in ¼-inch-thick slices**
- 3 **tablespoons chicken broth**

In a bowl, combine the ¼ cup chicken broth, vinegar, sugar, salt, and cornstarch.

Heat a wok or wide frying pan over high heat. When pan is hot, add oil. When oil is hot, add carrots and onion and stir-fry for 1 minute. Add the 3 tablespoons chicken broth, cover, and reduce heat to medium. Cook until carrot is crisp-tender (about 4 minutes). Increase heat to high. Stir cornstarch mixture once, add to pan and cook, stirring, until sauce bubbles and thickens. Makes 4 servings.

After you savor Green Pepper Beef (recipe on page 40), break apart the crisp Phoenix Nest (recipe on page 76) and nibble. This nest is made with yams.

Cold Spiced Cabbage

Peking

This mildly spiced relish makes a fine addition to a cold appetizer selection. Or you could serve it in little dishes for nibbling between rich spicy courses.

- 1 **small head (about 1½ lbs.) Chinese cabbage (napa cabbage) or regular cabbage**
- 2 **tablespoons salad oil**
- 2 **cloves garlic, minced**
- ⅓ **cup water**
- 3 **tablespoons** *each* **sugar and white wine vinegar**
- ½ **teaspoon salt**
- 1½ **teaspoons sesame oil**
- ¼ **to ½ teaspoon crushed red pepper**

Cut cabbage in 2-inch squares; you should have about 8 cups. Heat a wok or wide frying pan over high heat. When pan is hot, add oil. When oil begins to heat, add garlic and stir once around pan. Add cabbage and stir-fry for 30 seconds. Add water, cover, and cook, stirring occasionally, until cabbage just barely wilts (about 1½ minutes). Remove from heat and pour off any excess liquid.

Stir sugar, vinegar, salt, sesame oil, and red pepper into cabbage. Cool, cover, and refrigerate up to a week. Serve cold. Makes about 2½ cups.

Broccoli with Chicken

Shanghai

This vegetable dish, combined with chicken, is hearty enough to make a meal. Instead of stir-frying the chicken and broccoli together in one pan, you cook them separately to serve side by side. As a result, each ingredient retains its own identity and delicate flavor. At another time, you could substitute bok choy, green beans, or asparagus for the broccoli. The important thing is to cook the vegetables just to the crisp-tender stage.

- 1 **tablespoon** *each* **soy sauce, cornstarch, and water**
- ¼ **teaspoon salt**
- ½ **teaspoon** *each* **sesame oil and sugar**
- ⅛ **teaspoon white pepper**
- 1 **pound chicken breasts, skinned, boned, and cut in bite-size pieces**
- 3 **tablespoons salad oil Cooking sauce (directions follow)**
- 1 **pound broccoli Vegetable cooking water (directions follow)**
- 1 **clove garlic, minced**
- ½ **teaspoon minced fresh ginger**
- 1 **whole green onion, thinly sliced**

In a bowl, combine soy, cornstarch, water, salt, sesame oil, sugar, and pepper. Add chicken and toss to coat. Stir in 1 tablespoon of the salad oil. Let stand for 15 minutes to marinate.

Prepare cooking sauce and set aside.

Cut off broccoli flowerets in 3-inch lengths. Peel thick stalks, then thinly slice. Boil vegetable cooking water, add broccoli, and cook until crisp-tender (about 3 minutes). Drain, then discard green onion and ginger. Arrange broccoli on opposite ends of a serving dish. Keep warm.

Heat a wok or wide frying pan over high heat. When pan is hot, add the remaining 2 tablespoons salad oil. When oil begins to heat, add garlic and ginger. Stir once, then add chicken and stir-fry until chicken is opaque (about 3 minutes). Stir cooking sauce, add to pan along with green onion, and cook, stirring, until sauce bubbles and thickens. Spoon onto center of serving dish. Makes 4 servings.

Cooking sauce. In a bowl, combine ¼ cup **chicken broth**, 1 teaspoon **cornstarch**, ½ teaspoon **dry sherry**, and ¼ teaspoon *each* **salt** and **sesame oil.**

Vegetable cooking water. In a large pan combine 4 cups **water**, 2 dime-size slices fresh **ginger** (crushed with the side of a cleaver), 1 whole **green onion**, 2 tablespoons **salad oil**, 1 tablespoon *each* **dry sherry** and **sugar**, and 1 teaspoon **salt.**

Rice, Noodles & Doughs

Geographical location often determines the staple food of a region, and this is very evident in China. Fragrant steamed rice is the basic starch in the warm regions of the south. The colder climate of the north is more suitable for growing wheat. From there come crisp breads, steamed buns, soft dumplings, and silky noodles. But the Chinese don't limit themselves to one thing, and each region has developed its own specialties based on rice, wheat, and other grains.

The Canton area is famous for dozens of little savory dishes called *dim sum*—literally translated "dot heart." You order dim sum in a tea house, and as food is wheeled by your table on a tea cart, you can select a little or a lot.

One of the delights of Chinese eating is the flexibility of foods. Many of the dishes in this chapter can serve as part of a Chinese menu, but they are equally at home, in the Western sense, as appetizers, snacks, and single-entrée meals.

Steamed Rice

The typical partner of Chinese food is a bowl of steamed rice. For daily meals, it is the staple—to be embroidered with little savory dishes that tease the palate. The Chinese prefer long-grain rice that cooks up fluffy and dry, and they cook it without salt to provide a neutral base for each seasoned accompaniment.

Measure 1 cup **long-grain rice** into a 2-quart pan and wash with water (to remove excess starch) until water runs clear; drain. Add 1½ cups cold **water** and boil, uncovered, over medium-high heat until water and bubbles disappear from the surface (about 8 minutes). Cover pan, turn heat to low, and steam until rice is soft (about 20 minutes). Turn off heat and let rice sit for 5 minutes or up to 30 minutes. Fluff with a fork before serving. Makes 4 servings.

Shrimp Fried Rice

(Pictured on page 83)

In home-style cooking, fried rice provides an easy way to convert bits of leftovers into a quick snack or one-dish meal. The embellishments are flexible; the rule for rice is not—you must start with cold, cooked rice so the grains remain separate when stir-fried.

- 4 cups cold, cooked long-grain rice (1¼ cups uncooked rice)
- 2 eggs
- ¼ teaspoon salt
- 4 tablespoons salad oil
- 2 whole green onions, thinly sliced
- 1 cup small cooked shrimp or 1 cup diced barbecued pork (page 17), or cooked ham or chicken
- ½ cup frozen peas, thawed
- ½ cup roasted cashew nuts
- 2 tablespoons soy sauce
- ½ teaspoon salt

Rub cooked rice with wet hands so all the grains are separated. Beat eggs with the ¼ teaspoon salt. In a wok or wide frying pan, heat 1 tablespoon of the oil over medium heat. Add green onion and stir-fry for about 30 seconds. Add eggs and stir and cook until soft curds form; remove from pan and set aside.

Heat another tablespoon oil in pan. Add shrimp, peas, and cashews. Stir-fry for 2 minutes to heat through; remove from pan and set aside. Heat the remaining 2 tablespoons oil in pan. Add rice and stir-fry for 2 minutes to heat through. Stir in soy and shrimp mixture. Add eggs and fold in until they are in small pieces. Season with salt. Makes 4 or 5 servings.

Sizzling Rice

In a cuisine that wastes little, Chinese cooks have devised many imaginative dishes. Sizzling rice is one of them. When rice is cooked, the crust that forms on the bottom of the pot is dried and deep-fried for sizzling dishes such as sizzling rice soup (page 27) or sizzling sweet and sour seafood (page 62). It takes time to save enough rice crusts, but you can start from scratch and easily make a quantity to use for several dishes. Start with short-grain rice—because it cooks up rather sticky, the rice will stay in a layer as it dries.

Place 1 cup **short-grain rice** in a 2-quart pan. Wash with water until water runs clear; drain. Add 1 cup cold **water.** Cover and bring to a boil over high heat; reduce heat to low and simmer for 20 minutes. Turn off heat and let stand for 30 minutes. Turn rice into a wide frying pan (preferably with a nonstick finish); pack in an even layer about ½-inch thick. Cook over low heat for 1 hour. Turn layer of rice over and cook for another hour or until rice is very dry. When cool, break into 2-inch squares and store in an airtight container, at room temperature, up to 3 months.

To cook sizzling rice, pour **salad oil** to a depth of 1 inch in a small deep pan. Heat to 375° on a deep-frying thermometer. Cook rice squares, 2 or 3 at a time, until

golden (about 2 minutes). Drain briefly on paper towels, then use while still hot in any sizzling dish.

Chinese Rice Soup

For breakfast or snacks—never as a soup course—the Chinese eat a creamy rice soup (also called *congee* or *jook*) topped with an assortment of tasty relishes. Flavorful and filling, it is a fine choice for a Western lunch or supper.

> 2 **quarts chicken broth, page 24 or canned**
> ¾ **cup uncooked rice (short or long grain)**
> ¾ **pound uncooked boneless lean meat, such as beef (top round or flank steak), pork (shoulder or butt), or chicken**
> 1 **tablespoon** *each* **salad oil, dry sherry, and soy sauce**
> **About 2 cups coarsely chopped lettuce**
> **About ½ cup thinly sliced whole green onions**
> **About ¼ cup coarsely chopped fresh coriander (also called Chinese parsley or cilantro)**
> **Soy sauce**

Combine broth and rice in a 5-quart or larger heavy pan. Bring to a boil; reduce heat, cover, and simmer, stirring occasionally, for 1½ hours.

Meanwhile, slice meat in ¼-inch-thick strips that are about 1 by 2 inches. In a bowl mix the meat with oil, sherry, and soy. When soup is thick, stir in meat; cover and cook until meat is no longer pink inside (about 5 minutes for beef or chicken, 15 minutes for pork). Ladle soup into bowls. Pass lettuce, green onion, coriander, and soy to garnish individual servings. Makes 6 servings.

Chinese Noodles

You cannot explore Chinese cooking for long without discovering noodles in all sizes and shapes. Wheat and egg noodles form the

basic starch in northern China. Noodles made from rice are more common in the eastern and southern regions.

In our markets you can easily find noodles to prepare Chinese-style. Fresh noodles are best, so if you see them in the market you might want to buy several bags (they freeze well)—but dried thin noodles or a thin spaghetti make a good substitute.

To cook noodles, heat a large pan of **water** to boiling. Drop in **fresh or dried noodles** and stir to separate the strands. When water comes to a boil, add ½ cup cold water. When water boils again, cook for about 3 minutes for fresh noodles, 7 to 9 minutes for the dried ones. Do not overcook—like Italian pasta, noodles should still have a bite to them. Drain in a colander and rinse with cold water.

For each pound of noodles, stir in 1 tablespoon **sesame oil** or salad oil and 1 tablespoon **soy sauce** or ½ teaspoon salt. Use immediately or refrigerate in a covered container for a day or two. Reheat by dipping in hot water or hot broth, or by pan-frying.

注意 **One-piece noodle soup.** Nestle **cooked noodles** in bowls of steaming **chicken or pork broth** and garnish with slivers of **cooked chicken,** slices of **hard-cooked egg,** thinly sliced **Chinese cabbage** (napa cabbage) or iceberg lettuce, and thinly sliced **green onion.**

注意 **Cold-stirred noodles.** Serve chilled and drained **cooked noodles** in bowls topped with sliced **barbecued pork** (page 17), **bean sprouts** (blanched for 30 seconds and chilled), and thinly sliced **cucumber, radish,** and **green onion.** Pass **soy sauce, vinegar, sesame oil,** and **chili oil** so each person can season and toss to taste.

注意 **Pan-fried noodles.** (Pictured on page 58) In a wide frying pan (preferably with a nonstick finish), heat 2 tablespoons **salad oil** over medium-high heat.

Spread drained, cooked noodles in a layer 1 inch thick. Cook until golden brown. Turn noodles over in one piece, add another tablespoon **salad oil,** and brown the other side. Cut in wedges or serve whole, topped with any stir-fried meat or vegetable dish.

Filled Fresh Rice Noodles

In Chinese noodle factories, long sheets of rice noodles are pressed out between rollers like lengths of fabric. The housewife buys them in small sections, either to stuff with a filling the way we would fill crêpes, or to cut into strips and heat through in a soup or a stir-fried dish. Using cake flour in place of rice flour, you can duplicate them easily at home without any special equipment.

> 1 **cup unsifted cake flour**
> 1 **tablespoon cornstarch**
> ½ **teaspoon salt**
> 1¼ **cups cold water**
> 2 **tablespoons salad oil**
> **Filling (directions follow)**
> **Soy sauce**
> **Sesame oil or sesame seeds**

In a bowl, mix flour, cornstarch, and salt. Combine water and oil; pour into flour and blend until smooth and no lumps remain. Ladle ⅓ cup batter into a lightly greased 9-inch pie pan. Place pan on a level rack in a steamer, cover, and steam over boiling water for 5 minutes.

Remove pan from steamer and set in a baking pan filled with water and ice cubes to hasten cooling. When cool, loosen edges from pie pan with the tip of a knife and roll up jelly roll style. Wipe pan clean with a paper towel, grease lightly, and repeat until all the batter is used. For faster cooking, you can use two pie pans so one can be steaming while another cools.

Cover noodles and keep at room temperature in a cool place for as long as 8 hours. To serve, unroll noodles and distribute filling equally over each circle. Roll after filling. Cut each roll in 1½-inch long sections and arrange on a serving platter. Drizzle over a few drops soy sauce and sesame oil or sesame seeds. Makes 5 rolls.

Filling. Prepare the following: ½ cup **Chinese barbecued pork** (page 17) or cooked ham, cut in matchstick pieces; **egg slivers** made from 2 eggs (page 25); ¼ pound **bean sprouts,** cooked in boiling water for 10 seconds, drained, rinsed in cold water, and chilled; and 2 whole **green onions,** cut in 1½-inch lengths and cut in thin lengthwise slices.

Bean Threads with Hot Bean Sauce

Szechwan

Glistening bean threads flecked with bits of pork look innocent enough, but prepared this way they absorb a fiery flavor from the Szechwan-style seasonings. The Chinese call this dish "ants climbing a tree."

> 2 **ounces dried bean threads**
> 2 **medium-size dried mushrooms**
> 3 **tablespoons salad oil**
> 1 **teaspoon minced fresh ginger**
> 2 **cloves garlic, minced**
> 2 **ounces boneless lean pork, finely chopped or ground**
> 1 **to 2 teaspoons hot bean sauce or 1 or 2 small, dry, hot chile peppers, crumbled and seeded, if desired**
> 1 **whole green onion, thinly sliced**
> ½ **cup chicken broth, page 24 or canned**
> 1 **tablespoon *each* dry sherry and soy sauce**
> 1 **teaspoon sesame oil**

Cover bean threads with warm water, let stand for 30 minutes, then drain. Place on a cutting board and cut in 4-inch lengths. Cover mushrooms with warm water, let stand for 30 minutes, then drain. Cut off and discard stems; squeeze mushrooms dry and thinly slice.

Heat a wok or wide frying pan over high heat. When pan is hot, add oil. When oil begins to heat, add ginger and garlic. Stir once, then add pork and hot bean sauce. Stir-fry until pork loses its pinkness (about 2 minutes). Reduce heat to medium. Add mushrooms, bean threads, green onion, chicken broth, sherry, and soy. Stirring occasionally, simmer until all liquid is absorbed (about 5 minutes). Stir in sesame oil just before serving. Makes 4 servings.

Fried Bean Threads & Rice Sticks

Like the tiny Chinese paper flowers that immediately "bloom" when dropped in a basin of water, dried bean threads and rice sticks puff and expand the second you drop them into hot fat.

In Chinese cooking, these crisp fried noodles are used as a garnish. Try them in Chinese chicken salad (page 49) or scatter a handful over a stir-fried dish to create a picture: Sprinkle crunchy white bean threads over stir-fried shrimp and you have created shrimp under snow; pile rice sticks, which turn golden when fried, on a stir-fried vegetable and you have vegetables under straw.

Bean threads and rice sticks are packaged in tight bundles and are messy to separate. To avoid scattering, place bundle in a large paper bag in which you pull the bundle apart into small sections or individual strands.

Pour salad oil into a wok or deep pan to a depth of 2 inches and heat to 375° on a deep-frying thermometer. Drop in one bean thread or rice stick. If it expands at once the oil is ready. Cook a handful at a time. As noodles puff and expand,

Golden cashews stud easy-to-make Shrimp Fried Rice (recipe on page 80). Marbled Tea Eggs (recipe on page 68) are hard-cooked eggs in disguise.

push them down into the oil with a wire strainer or slotted spoon, then turn over the entire mass to be sure all are cooked. When noodles stop crackling (about 30 seconds) remove with a strainer and drain on paper towels. After cooling, store in an airtight container (at room temperature) for up to a month.

Because the noodles are odorless and tasteless, you can recycle the cooking oil. Cool, strain, and refrigerate in a covered jar to use for general cooking or deep-frying.

Mandarin Pancakes
Peking   (Pictured on page 39)

These paper thin pancakes are the wrappers used to enclose succulent bites of Peking duck or mu shu pork. You can make them a day ahead or freeze them for longer storage.

> 2 **cups all-purpose flour, unsifted**
> ¾ **cup boiling water**
> **About 2 tablespoons sesame oil or salad oil**

Measure flour into a bowl and mix in water with a fork or chopsticks. Work dough several minutes until it holds together, then knead on a lightly floured board until smooth and satiny (about 10 minutes). Cover and let rest at room temperature for 30 minutes.

Roll dough into a 12-inch-long log. Cut into 12 equal pieces and keep covered.

To make each pancake, cut 1 piece of dough exactly in half. Roll each half into a ball and flatten slightly. Roll each ball on a very lightly floured board to a round 3 inches in diameter. Brush sesame oil lightly on top of one round and cover with another round. Press the 2 rounds lightly but firmly together.

Place the double round on a lightly floured board and roll out, from center to edges, until 7 or 8 inches in diameter (don't worry if rounds are not perfect). Turn frequently, brushing board lightly with flour as needed. Repeat procedure until you have 2 or 3 pancakes; then cook before making more.

Heat a wide frying pan over medium-high heat, then place a pancake on the ungreased surface. Turn about every 15 seconds until cake is blistered by air pockets, turns parchment color, and feels dry. Cake should not brown, but a few golden spots won't hurt. If overcooked, cake becomes brittle.

Remove from pan and carefully pull the two halves apart and stack them on a plate. Keep covered as you cook remaining cakes. Serve warm; or let cool, wrap airtight, and refrigerate or freeze for later use.

To heat for serving, thaw if frozen. Line a flat-bottomed steamer with a towel dipped in water and wrung dry; stack pancakes inside and fold towel over pancakes. Cover and steam over simmering water for 5 minutes. Fold hot pancakes in half, then in half again, and arrange in a serving basket. Since they dry out quickly, serve just a few at a time and keep remainder covered. Makes 24 pancakes.

Chinese Sesame Buns
Peking   (Pictured on page 86)

If you've ever tried to open a Chinese puzzle box, you know you must make a specific series of moves before you trigger the lock. In the same way, you must follow, in proper sequence, each step of folding and rolling this dough so it will puff and form a pocket during baking. The directions may sound complicated as you read them, but with dough in hand, the steps are easy and intriguing to follow.

Chinese doughs in a food processor

If you own a food processor, you can use it to make the mandarin pancakes, Chinese sesame buns, and green onion cakes found in this chapter, as well as the doughs for pork sui mai and pot stickers. None is difficult to mix by hand, but the processor does it quickly and cuts the kneading time roughly in half.

Fit the metal blade in the processor bowl, add the measured amount of flour (and salt if listed), and turn on the motor. Immediately pour the boiling water indicated in the recipe down the feed tube. Stop the machine as soon as the mixture forms a ball—if you continue to process you may overdevelop the gluten in the flour. Remove dough and knead lightly for a few minutes until it is smooth and satiny. (When you've mixed dough in the processor, it should not be necessary to flour the board for kneading.) Allow dough to rest for 30 minutes before following the rolling directions.

The crisp buns are delicious—good to eat plain, or to stuff with barbecued meat or with any stir-fried dish that doesn't have too much gravy. And the dough can be rolled ahead of time and frozen for a special meal.

2¼ **cups all-purpose flour, unsifted**
¼ **teaspoon salt**
1 **cup boiling water**
3 **tablespoons salad oil**
2 **tablespoons all-purpose flour**
About 3 tablespoons sesame seeds

In a bowl, combine the 2¼ cups flour and salt. Mix in water with a fork or chopsticks until dough is evenly moistened and begins to hold together. On a lightly floured board, knead dough, adding flour (as little as possible) to keep it from sticking, until very smooth and satiny (about 10 minutes). Cover and let rest at room temperature for 30 minutes.

Meanwhile, prepare a roux: in a small heavy pan, heat salad oil over medium heat until it flows freely. Add the 2 tablespoons flour and cook, stirring, just until mixture turns caramel color. Let cool.

To roll and shape sesame buns, follow the illustrations at right.
1. On a lightly floured board, roll dough out into an 8 by 15-inch rectangle. Spread cooled roux over dough. Cut rectangle crosswise into thirds. 2. Stack cut pieces on top of one another with roux-coated surfaces inside stack. (Some roux will ooze out.) 3. Cut stack in half lengthwise, and then crosswise into 4 equal pieces. You will now have 8 pieces. Don't worry if some corners are slightly rounded. 4. Roll each piece to ⅛-inch thickness, then fold 2 opposite sides toward center.
5. Overlap side, completely.
6. With seam side up, roll only half of each folded piece to ⅛-inch thickness. 7. Starting at thicker end, fold dough over twice toward thin end. 8. With thin end on top, dip bottom surface in sesame seeds. 9. With seed side up, roll out each bun to form a 3 by 5-inch rectangle ¼ inch thick. Place on

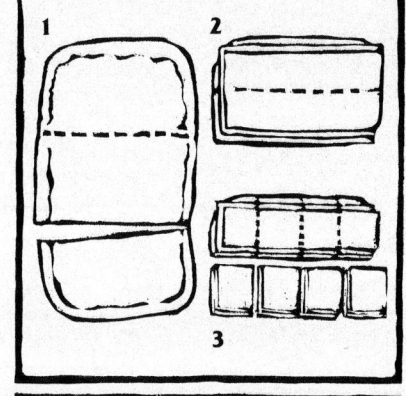

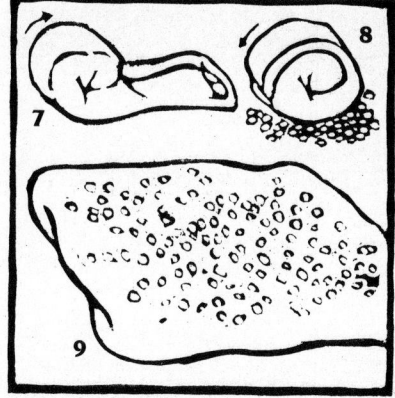

ungreased cooky sheet, seed side up. Let buns rest for at least 5 minutes before baking.

At this point you can cover and chill buns up to 24 hours; freeze for longer storage. Bake on the bottom rack of a 400° oven until golden brown and puffy (about 15 minutes if dough is at room temperature, 25 minutes if cold; frozen dough should be thawed before baking). If you plan to serve buns with a filling, slit 2 short sides and 1 long side open with scissors or a sharp knife; insert filling. Serve hot. Makes 8.

Pork-filled Buns

If you have ever visited a Chinese bakery or tea house, you may have noticed these unassuming smooth white buns. The Chinese name for them is *bow*. Inside, there's a savory meat filling.

Traditionally, bow are steamed and served hot as a snack or for dim sum. But modern Chinese cooks also bake them for the slightly different taste they add to a Chinese meal. Though steamed buns are always served hot, the baked buns are good hot or cold; both types can be made ahead and frozen.

With the same yeast dough, you can also make plain steamed buns, a favorite accompaniment for red-cooked (braised) meats and poultry.

1 **package active dry yeast**
1 **cup warm water (about 110°)**
⅓ **cup sugar**
2 **tablespoons salad oil**
1 **teaspoon salt**
About 3¼ cups all-purpose flour, unsifted
Pork filling (directions follow)
Melted butter or margarine

In a large bowl, dissolve yeast in water; blend in sugar, oil, and salt. Let stand in a warm place until bubbly (about 15 minutes). Add 3¼ cups of flour and mix until dough holds together. Place dough on a lightly floured board and knead until smooth and elastic (about 8 to 10 minutes). Place in a greased bowl, cover, and let rise in a warm place until doubled in bulk (about 1 hour and 15 minutes).

Meanwhile prepare pork filling; let cool and set aside.

Turn dough out onto a lightly floured board and knead for 1 minute. Shape into a rectangle. With a floured knife, cut rectangle in half lengthwise, then cut crosswise 6 times to make 12 equal pieces.

Roll each piece into a round about 4½ inches in diameter. Press outside edges of dough to make them slightly thinner than the rest of the round. Place about 2 tablespoons filling in center of each

round. Pull edges of dough up around filling and twist to seal as shown below.

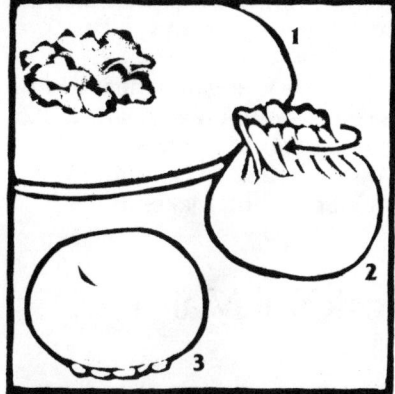

For steamed buns, place each bun, sealed side down, on a 3-inch square of foil. Cover and let rise in a warm place until puffy and light (about 30 minutes). Set in steamer over boiling water. Cover and steam for 12 to 15 minutes. (When done, tops of buns should be glazed and smooth.) Serve warm; or let cool, wrap, and freeze. To reheat, steam frozen buns until hot (about 10 minutes).

For baked buns, place buns about 2 inches apart on a greased cooky sheet. Cover and let rise in a warm place until puffy and light (about 30 minutes). Brush tops with melted butter and bake in a 350° oven until golden brown (about 15 minutes). Makes 12 buns.

Pork filling. Cut 1½ pounds **boneless lean pork** into ½-inch cubes. Season with 2 cloves **garlic** (minced), ½ teaspoon grated fresh **ginger,** 2 teaspoons **sugar,** and 2 tablespoons **soy sauce.** In a bowl, combine 2 teaspoons **sugar,** 1 tablespoon **cornstarch,** 2 tablespoons **soy sauce,** 1 tablespoon **dry sherry,** and ¼ cup **water;** reserve.

Heat 1 tablespoon **salad oil** in a wok or wide frying pan over high

Stuff a Chinese Sesame Bun (recipe on page 84) with a savory filling and eat it like a sandwich. Chicken with Peking Sauce (at left; recipe on page 46) is sweet and spicy; Yu-shiang Pork (in foreground; recipe on page 35) is hot and spicy.

heat. When oil is hot, add pork and stir-fry until browned (about 5 minutes). Add 1 medium-size chopped **onion** and continue stir-frying until onion is limp (about 2 minutes). Stir cornstarch mixture, add to pork, and cook, stirring, until sauce bubbles and thickens. Cool.

注意 **Steamed buns**—no filling. (Pictured on page 7) Prepare dough following directions for pork-filled buns, but eliminate filling. Shape dough into 12 round buns and place each on a foil square. Let rise for 30 minutes, then steam for 12 to 15 minutes.

Won Ton

Won ton can be presented many ways. First you wrap a filling in squares of noodle dough. Then you deep fry them for appetizers or dessert (page 92), or cook them in water to add to soup or to eat as dumplings with a spicy peanut sauce. The wrappers or skins are available, fresh or frozen, in 1-pound packages containing 60 to 70 squares.

Our directions show you the prettiest way to fill and wrap won ton for deep-frying. A less traditional way, but faster for soup or dumplings, is to dot the filling in the center of the skin, then pull the edges around it, moisten with egg, and squeeze slightly to seal.

1 **pound boneless lean pork, finely chopped or ground, or ½ pound** *each* **ground pork and medium-size raw shrimp, shelled, deveined, and finely chopped**
⅓ **cup water chestnuts, finely chopped**
2 **whole green onions, finely chopped**
1 **tablespoon soy sauce**
½ **teaspoon salt**
⅛ **teaspoon pepper**
½ **teaspoon minced fresh ginger**
2 **teaspoons dry sherry**
1 **egg**
1 **package (1 lb.) won ton skins**

Combine pork (and shrimp, if you use it), water chestnuts, onion,

soy, salt, pepper, ginger, and sherry until well mixed. Beat egg in a small bowl.

To wrap filling in won ton skin, follow the illustration below.

1. Place a won ton skin on the counter. (Cover remaining skins with a damp towel to keep them pliable.) Mound 1 teaspoon filling in one corner. **2.** Fold that corner over filling, and roll to tuck point under. Moisten the two side corners with egg. **3.** Bring side corners together, overlapping slightly. Pinch together firmly to seal. Place filled won ton on a baking sheet and cover while you fill the remaining skins; place slightly apart.

At this point you can refrigerate won ton up to 8 hours before cooking. Won ton for soup or dumplings can also be frozen before cooking. Freeze firm on a baking sheet, then transfer to plastic bags and return to freezer. Fried won ton can be frozen too, but it should be done after deep-frying. Cook won ton according to the following directions. Makes 6 to 7 dozen won ton.

Fried won ton. (Pictured on page 23) In a deep pan (at least 6 inches in diameter), pour **salad oil** to a depth of 2 inches and heat to 360° on a deep-frying thermometer. Fry 4 to 6 prepared **won ton** at a time, turning occasionally, for 2 minutes or until golden brown. Remove with a slotted spoon and drain on paper towels. Keep warm in a 200° oven until all are cooked, then serve with a dipping sauce of **hot mustard** (page 37), catsup, or sweet and pungent sauce (page 48). If cooked ahead, cool fried won ton, then freeze in plastic bags. To reheat, arrange in a single layer (while still frozen) on a baking sheet and heat in a 350° oven for 12 minutes.

Won ton soup. Count on 1 cup **chicken broth,** 1 sliced **green onion,** ¼ cup coarsely sliced **Chinese cabbage** (napa cabbage) or bok choy, and 6 to 8 **won ton** for each serving. Heat broth in a pan. When simmering, add green onion and cabbage and cook for 3 minutes. Meanwhile, drop about 15 filled won ton (fresh or frozen) at a time into a large pan of boiling water. After they rise to the surface, simmer until filling is no longer pink (about 4 minutes, or 6 minutes if frozen). Remove with a slotted spoon and drop into hot broth. Garnish each serving with 1 or 2 slices of **barbecued pork** (page 17) and season with a few drops of **soy sauce** and **sesame oil.**

注意 **Won ton dumplings with spicy peanut sauce.** Allow 10 to 12 **won ton** for each entrée serving, 6 for a first-course serving. Cook filled won ton (fresh or frozen) in boiling water, following directions for won ton soup. Drain well and turn into individual bowls. Serve hot and pass **spicy peanut sauce** (page 48) to pour over hot dumplings.

Green Onion Cakes

Peking   (Pictured on page 31)

Like a tortilla, this unleavened bread is thin and chewy. The northern Chinese serve it as a change from rice. In Western menus, it makes a delicious appetizer or accompaniment to soup or salad.

    1   **cup all-purpose flour, unsifted**
    ½   **teaspoon salt**
    ⅓   **cup boiling water**
    4   **strips bacon**
    2   **whole green onions, thinly sliced**
        About 3 tablespoons sesame seeds
    1   **tablespoon salad oil**

In a bowl, combine flour and salt. Mix in water with a fork or chopsticks until dough is evenly moistened and begins to hold together. On a lightly floured board, knead dough until smooth and satiny (about 3 minutes). Cover dough and let rest at room temperature for 30 minutes.

Meanwhile, in a frying pan over medium heat, cook bacon until crisp; drain (reserve drippings) and crumble.

On a lightly floured board, roll dough into a rectangle 8 by 16 inches. To shape, follow illustrations below. **1.** Cut dough crosswise in eight 2-inch-wide

strips. Brush each strip with ½ teaspoon bacon drippings, then sprinkle almost to the edges with bacon and green onion. **2.** Starting with a short end, roll up each strip jelly roll style; pinch seam across top to seal. **3.** Stand roll on work surface. Flatten into a circle with your palm. **4.** Roll circle into a disk about 4 inches in diameter. If filling begins to come out, press back into dough. Sprinkle about

½ teaspoon sesame seeds on each side of circle and lightly press into dough. At this point you can stack rounds (separate with sheets of wax paper), cover, and chill for up to 8 hours.

In a wide frying pan, heat salad oil over medium-high heat. Cook several cakes at a time until golden brown (about 2 to 3 minutes on a side). Serve hot. Makes 8.

Pork Sui Mai

Canton

A favorite kind of dim sum, these tiny open-faced steamed dumplings make a wonderful beginning for a Chinese meal. You can use won ton wrappers for the dough, or make your own with the directions that follow.

    4   **medium-size dried mushrooms or**
        ½ cup minced fresh mushrooms
    2   **cups (about 1 lb.) finely chopped**
        or ground boneless lean pork
    ⅓   **cup minced green onion**
    ¼   **cup *each* minced water chestnuts**
        and bamboo shoots
    2   **teaspoons minced fresh**
        coriander (also called Chinese
        parsley or cilantro)
    1   **teaspoon grated fresh ginger**
    3   **tablespoons soy sauce**
    1½ **tablespoons cornstarch**
    1   **egg white**
    4   **dozen won ton skins or sui mai**
        dumpling dough (directions
        follow)
    1   **small carrot, grated**
        Salad oil
        Soy sauce

Cover mushrooms with warm water, let stand for 30 minutes, then drain. Cut off and discard stems; squeeze mushrooms dry and finely chop. Mix mushrooms with pork, onion, water chestnuts, bamboo shoots, coriander, and ginger. Blend the 3 tablespoons soy with cornstarch and add to pork mixture along with egg white. Stir until well mixed. Divide mixture into 48 equal balls.

To make each dumpling, cut off corners of won ton skin to form a circle, or roll a piece of dumpling dough out on a very lightly floured board to make a 3-inch circle. Place a pork ball on center of dough. Crumple dough up and around filling and give a light squeeze in the middle—top surface of filling should be exposed. Tap bottom on a flat surface so dumpling will stand upright. Put ¼ teaspoon carrot in center of each dumpling. See illustration below. Brush dumpling with salad oil.

Keep covered until all are shaped.

Place dumplings, without crowding, on a greased rack that will fit inside a steamer, wok, or deep pan. Pour boiling water into steamer, leaving 1½ inches between water level and rack. Cover and steam for 20 minutes.

Serve dumplings hot or, if cooked ahead, cover and chill for up to 1 day or freeze for up to 1 month. To freeze cooked dumplings, place slightly apart on a baking sheet and freeze until firm, then transfer to plastic bags and return to freezer. Set dumplings apart to thaw; they stick if they touch. Reheat by steaming for 5 minutes. Serve with soy sauce for dipping. Makes 4 dozen dumplings.

Sui mai dumpling dough. Measure 1 cup unsifted **all-purpose flour** into a bowl. Mix in ½ cup **boiling water** with a fork or chopsticks. Work dough several minutes until it holds together, then knead on a lightly floured board until smooth and velvety (about 10 minutes). Cover and let rest at room temper-

ature for 30 minutes.

Roll dough into a log 24 inches long, cut log into 1-inch lengths, then cut each length in half to make 48 pieces. Keep remaining pieces covered to prevent drying as you shape each dumpling according to directions at left.

Pot Stickers
Peking

The northern Chinese eat these savory dumplings as a snack, but they are so tasty and substantial you could pair them with soup or salad for a meal. They're called pot stickers only because they look as if they'll stick to the pan, but you can easily scoop them up with a spatula.

    Shrimp filling (directions follow)
3 cups all-purpose flour, unsifted
¼ teaspoon salt
1 cup boiling water
    About ¼ cup salad oil
    About 1⅓ cups chicken broth, page 24 or canned
    Soy sauce, vinegar, and chili oil

Prepare shrimp filling and set aside. In a bowl, combine flour and salt. Mix in water with a fork or chopsticks until dough is evenly moistened and begins to hold together. On an unfloured board, knead dough until it is very smooth and satiny (about 5 minutes). Cover and let rest at room temperature for 30 minutes.

Divide dough into 2 equal portions. Keeping one portion covered to prevent drying; roll out other portion until it is about 14 inches in diameter and ⅛ inch thick. Cut out 3½ to 4-inch circles with a round cooky cutter or a clean can with ends removed.

Dot each circle with about 2 teaspoons filling. To shape each pot sticker, fold dough in half over filling to form a half moon. Pinch closed about ½ inch of the curved edges. As you continue to seal edges, form 3 tucks along the dough edge facing you, as shown at the top of the next column. Continue pressing edges together

until entire curve is sealed. Set pot sticker down firmly, seam side up, so that dumpling will sit flat. Cover while you shape remaining pot stickers.

If made ahead, freeze pot stickers in a single layer on a baking sheet until firm; then transfer to plastic bags and freeze for up to a month. Cook without thawing, as directed below.

Cook pot stickers a dozen at a time. For each batch, heat 1 tablespoon oil in a heavy, wide frying pan over medium heat. Set pot stickers, seam side up, in pan. Cook until bottoms are golden brown (about 8 to 10 minutes). Pour in ⅓ cup broth and immediately cover pan tightly. Reduce heat to low and steam pot stickers for 10 minutes (15 minutes if frozen). Uncover and continue cooking until all liquid is absorbed. Using a wide spatula to remove pot stickers from pan, place them, browned-side-up, on a serving platter. Serve hot, with soy, vinegar, and chili oil on the side. Makes about 4 dozen pot stickers, about 6 to 10 servings.

Shrimp filling. Chop ½ pound shelled and deveined **medium-size raw shrimp**. Mix with ½ pound finely chopped or ground **boneless lean pork,** 1 cup finely shredded **cabbage,** ¼ cup *each* minced **green onion** and chopped **fresh mushrooms,** 1 clove **garlic** (minced), ½ teaspoon **salt,** and 2 tablespoons **oyster sauce** or soy sauce. Makes enough to fill 4 dozen pot stickers.

Sweet Dishes

In a Chinese meal, the dessert rarely steals the show. The daily meal at home ends without a sweet, and the menus of most Chinese restaurants, which offer dozens of savory main dishes, list only a few simple desserts.

Still, the Chinese enjoy sweets. They nibble on them as snacks with tea, and elaborate desserts are presented as banquet fare.

The absence of a grand finale may pose a problem to the Western cook who likes to round out a menu with dessert. In this chapter we bow to tradition and offer some delicious ways to conclude a Chinese meal.

A lychee sundae or an anise pear compote is refreshing after a meal of many flavors, and Chinese pastries provide make-ahead convenience as well as good eating. Spectacular fried apples or bananas are worth the last-minute preparation if you match them with an easy menu. And a platter of fruit, such as sliced melon, peaches, mandarin oranges, lychees, or kumquats, is always in keeping with the spirit of a Chinese meal.

Caramel Fried Apples or Bananas

Peking   (Pictured on page 94)

Cooking this unusual dessert is definitely dramatic, and fascinating for guests to watch in the kitchen. Caramelizing the sugar calls for split second timing—it goes so quickly that you don't have time to use a candy thermometer. In fact, you may want to practice this step once before making the whole dessert.

We also offer bananas with sesame-peanut topping, a dessert from Hunan which begins the same way but ends in a more leisurely fashion.

- ½ cup all-purpose flour, unsifted
- 2 tablespoons cornstarch
- ¾ teaspoon baking powder
- ½ cup water
- 2 Golden Delicious apples or 2 bananas
   Salad oil
   Caramel coating: ⅔ cup granulated sugar, ⅓ cup warm water, and 1 tablespoon salad oil
- 2 teaspoons sesame seeds

In a bowl, mix flour, cornstarch, and baking powder. Add water and stir until smooth. Peel and core apples; cut each apple into 8 wedges. (If you use bananas, peel and cut in ½-inch-thick diagonal slices.) Place fruit in batter and turn to coat evenly.

Into a deep pan (about 6 inches in diameter), pour oil to a depth of about 1½ inches. Heat oil to 350° on a deep-frying thermometer. Using chopsticks or a spoon, lift 1 piece of fruit at a time from batter and let excess batter drip off, then lower fruit into hot oil. Cook several pieces at a time until coating is golden brown (about 2 minutes). Remove with a slotted spoon and drain on paper towels.

Generously oil a flat serving dish. Fill a serving bowl to the brim with ice cubes; cover with water.

Place sugar, water, and oil for caramel coating in a 10-inch frying pan; stir to blend. Place pan over high heat. When mixture begins to

A mélange of fresh fruit flavored with anise (recipe on page 93) is a refreshing way to end a Chinese meal. For the sweet tooth, serve Chinese Rosettes (recipe on page 92).

bubble (about 1 minute), shake pan continuously to prevent burning. Continue cooking and shaking pan until syrup *just* turns a pale straw color (about 9 minutes). Immediately remove from heat, add sesame seeds, and swirl to mix. (Syrup will continue to cook after you remove it from heat and color will turn golden in a few seconds.) Drop fruit into syrup and swirl to coat evenly. Using two spoons, immediately remove each piece of fruit and place on oiled dish so pieces do not touch. At table, dip each piece of fruit in ice water so coating hardens and fruit cools. Makes 6 servings.

注意 **Bananas with sesame-peanut topping.** Place 2 teaspoons **sesame seeds** in a heavy frying pan. Shaking pan, heat over medium heat until seeds turn golden and begin to pop (about 2 minutes); cool. Combine with ¼ cup finely chopped **peanuts** and ¼ cup **sugar;** set aside.

Peel 2 **bananas** and cut in ¼-inch-thick diagonal slices. Coat with batter and deep-fry according to preceding directions for caramel fried apples. Just before serving, sprinkle peanut topping over hot bananas. Makes 6 servings.

Chinese Rosettes

(Pictured on page 91)

Chinese cooks use rosette irons and an unusual batter to make these fanciful paper-thin pastries. Cookware shops sell the modestly priced irons singly or in sets with interchangeable designs.

- ½ cup cornstarch
- 2 tablespoons all-purpose flour
- 2 teaspoons sugar
- 1 teaspoon ground cinnamon
- ½ teaspoon salt
- 1 egg
- ¼ cup milk
  Salad oil
  Powdered sugar

In a bowl, mix cornstarch, flour, sugar, cinnamon, and salt. Beat egg slightly, combine with milk, and add to dry ingredients. Stir until batter is smooth.

Into a deep pan (about 6 inches in diameter), pour oil to a depth of about 1½ inches and heat to 375°

on a deep-frying thermometer. For each rosette, preheat iron in the oil; dip hot iron into batter nearly to, but not over, top of iron. (If batter does not adhere to iron, temperature of either iron or fat is too hot or too cold.)

Lower iron into oil for about 10 seconds or until rosette is lightly browned. Remove from oil, gently loosen rosette with a fork, and drain on paper towels. When completely cooled, sprinkle with powdered sugar. Store in an airtight container. Makes about 1½ dozen rosettes.

Date & Sesame Won Ton

There is more than one way to stuff won ton. Wrap a sweet filling inside, and the noodle squares become a delicious make-ahead dessert.

- ¼ cup sesame seeds
- ¼ cup firmly packed brown sugar
- ½ cup finely chopped pitted dates
- 1 tablespoon softened butter or margarine
- ½ package (1-lb. size) won ton skins
- 1 egg, lightly beaten
  Salad oil
  Powdered sugar

In a heavy frying pan over medium heat, toast sesame seeds, shaking pan occasionally, until they turn golden and begin to pop (about 2 minutes); cool. Crush seeds coarsely in a mortar. Combine with brown sugar, dates, and butter.

Fill and wrap won ton according to directions on page 87, using 1 teaspoon filling for each won ton and moistening edges with egg to seal.

Into a deep pan, pour oil to a depth of about 1½ inches and heat to 350° on a deep-frying thermometer. Fry 4 to 6 won ton at a time for 1 minute or until golden. Remove with a slotted spoon and drain on paper towels. When completely cooled, sprinkle with

powdered sugar. Store in an airtight container. Makes about 3 dozen won ton.

Almond Cream

A traditional recipe prepared in a modern way, this creamy pudding shows off best when served in stemmed glasses or clear sherbet dishes.

- 1 envelope unflavored gelatin
- 1 cup cold water
- ¼ cup sugar
- 2 cups half-and-half (light cream)
- 2 teaspoons almond extract
- 1 can (11 oz.) mandarin oranges, chilled

In a pan, sprinkle gelatin over water; let stand for 5 minutes to soften. Place over medium heat and, stirring, heat until gelatin dissolves. Add sugar and stir until it dissolves. Remove from heat and stir in half-and-half and almond extract. Pour into 6 small serving dishes and chill until firm (at least 4 hours). To serve, drain oranges and spoon over cream. Makes 6 servings.

Almond Cookies
Canton

The Chinese bake few desserts. Almond cookies—rich, tender, and not overly sweet—are among the delicious exceptions. For variety, you can crown the cookies with pine nuts, used in northern Chinese cooking, or with peanuts.

- 1 cup (½ lb.) lard or shortening
- ½ cup granulated sugar
- ¼ cup firmly packed brown sugar
- 1 egg
- 1 teaspoon almond extract
- 2¼ cups all-purpose flour, unsifted
- ⅛ teaspoon salt
- 1½ teaspoons baking powder
  About 5 dozen whole blanched almonds
- 1 egg yolk
- 2 tablespoons water

 # How to make a dragon-size fortune cooky

The cooky with the mysterious message inside is not authentically Chinese. But it tastes good and is a snap to make—especially in the giant, or dragon-size, version given here. Try it for a gift or to honor a special guest.

First write three fortunes on 1 by 3-inch strips of paper. Use wit or wisdom—even puns can be fun. Place fortunes and two pot holders near the oven for convenience.

In a bowl combine ½ cup unsifted **all-purpose flour,** 1 tablespoon **cornstarch,** ¼ cup **sugar,** and ¼ teaspoon **salt.** Blend in ¼ cup

salad oil. Add ¼ cup **egg whites** (about 2 large eggs), 1½ teaspoons **water,** and 1 teaspoon **vanilla;** stir until smooth.

Bake 1 cooky at a time. Drop ⅓ level cup of batter on a greased cooky sheet. Spread evenly into a 10-inch circle. Bake in a 300° oven until cooky turns a light golden brown (about 13 to 15 minutes).

Immediately place a fortune in center of hot, pliable cooky. Using pot holders to protect your hands, bring two opposite sides of cooky together, grasp ends of folded cooky, and gently pull together to crease. Hold folded cooky for a minute to maintain its shape as it finishes cooling and becomes crisp.

The baking temperature is the secret of these cookies. If the oven rises above 300°, the edges of the cooky will become overly brown and will crack when you fold it. When baked cookies are completely cool, store in an airtight container. Makes 3 giant fortune cookies.

Cream lard with granulated and brown sugar until fluffy. Add egg and almond extract; beat until well blended. Sift flour with salt and baking powder. Add to creamed mixture and blend well.

To shape each cooky, roll 1 tablespoon of mixture at a time into a ball. Place balls 2 inches apart on ungreased cooky sheets. Press down on each ball to make a 2-inch round. Press an almond in center of each round. Beat egg yolk and water; brush mixture over top of each cooky.

Bake in a 350° oven until lightly browned (about 10 to 12 minutes). Cool on wire racks. Store in an airtight container. Makes about 5 dozen cookies.

注意 **Sesame Cookies.** Follow directions for almond cookies, but substitute about ¼ cup **sesame seeds** for almonds. Press each ball in the palm of your hand to make a 2-inch round. Brush egg mixture on one side of each round, then dip coated side in sesame seeds. Place cookies, seed side up, on an ungreased cooky sheet and bake according to directions for almond cookies.

Lychee Ice Cream Sauce

Chinese cooks prize lychees for their exotic perfume as well as their fruity flavor. Dried in their tan leathery shells, lychees taste much like raisins and are pleasant for munching. Canned lychees are shelled, pitted, and juicy—ready to use in this fragrant sauce. Serve it over vanilla, toasted almond, or pineapple ice cream.

¼ **cup sugar**
1 **tablespoon cornstarch**
1 **can (1 lb. 4 oz.) lychees**
2 **teaspoons butter or margarine**
1 **tablespoon minced candied ginger**
2 **tablespoons lime juice**

Mix together sugar and cornstarch in a pan. Drain syrup from lychees (you should have 1 cup) and blend into cornstarch mixture. Add butter and ginger and cook, stirring, until sauce bubbles and thickens (about 2 minutes). Remove from heat and stir in lychees and lime juice. Serve warm or at room temperature spooned over ice cream. Makes 3 cups sauce.

Anise Pear Compote

(Pictured on page 91)

Any variety of fresh pears lends itself to this refreshing dessert. For the most traditional version, look for fresh Chinese snow pears in Oriental markets during the fall.

½ **cup sugar**
¾ **cup water**
¼ **teaspoon anise seeds, crushed**
1 **teaspoon lemon juice**
  Dash of salt
1½ **pounds firm ripe pears**
1 **large orange**
1 **grapefruit**
½ **cup seedless grapes**

In a medium-size pan, bring sugar, water, anise, lemon juice, and salt to a boil; reduce heat to simmer. Peel, quarter, and core pears. Place in hot syrup, cover, and simmer until barely tender when pierced (about 6 minutes); cool.

With a sharp knife, peel orange and grapefruit, remove white membrane, and lift out sections. Add orange and grapefruit sections and grapes to pears; gently mix. Chill. Makes 4 or 5 servings.

Index

Caramel Fried Apples (recipe on page 90) reflect the elegant cuisine of Peking. Dip hot fruit in ice water to cool and harden the golden coating.

A Handy Metric Conversion Table

To change	To	Multiply by
ounces (oz.)	grams (g)	28
pounds (lbs.)	kilograms (kg)	0.45
teaspoons	milliliters (ml)	5
tablespoons	milliliters (ml)	15
fluid ounces (fl. oz.)	milliliters (ml)	30
cups	liters (l)	0.24
pints (pt.)	liters (l)	0.45
quarts (qt.)	liters (l)	0.95
gallons (gal.)	liters (l)	3.8
inches	centimeters (cm)	2.5
Fahrenheit temperature (°F)	*Celsius temperature (°C)*	*5/9 after subtracting 32*